JEFFERSON'S "BIBLE"

THE
LIFE AND MORALS
OF
JESUS OF NAZARETH

BY THOMAS JEFFERSON

Foreword by William Murchison
and
Introduction by Judd W. Patton

AMERICAN BOOK DISTRIBUTORS
P.O. BOX 309
GROVE CITY, PA 16127-0309
(412) 458-5861

. . . .

PHOTOGRAPH CREDITS:
Front Cover:
Monticello/Thomas Jefferson Memorial Foundation, Inc.

John F. Lacey:
Major John F. Lacey, Iowa Park and Forestry Association, 1915

Cover Design:
Jon Brooks, Image Building Communications

. . . .

Library of Congress Cataloging-in-Publication Data:
Jefferson, Thomas, 1743-1826.
Jefferson's Bible/The Life and Morals of Jesus of Nazareth;
With a Foreword by William Murchison and
an Introduction by Judd W. Patton

Originally published:
Washington, D.C.: U.S.G.P.O.
1904

. . . .

ISBN 0-929205-02-2

JEFFERSON'S "BIBLE"

THE
LIFE AND MORALS
OF
JESUS OF NAZARETH

This special edition and reprint
of
The Jefferson "Bible"
is Dedicated to
America's Leaders
Past, Present, and Future

* * *

May our Present and Future Leaders
Carry Out Benjamin Franklin's 1778 Insight:

"Whoever shall introduce into public affairs the
principles of primitive Christianity will change
the face of the world."

CONTENTS

APPENDICES

FOREWORD

by William Murchison

Republication of the so-called "Jefferson Bible" comes at a poignant moment in American history: a moment Thomas Jefferson might find it hard to comprehend.

In the comparative serenity of early 19th century America, there was virtually no dispute over the centrality of religion to our national purposes. Religion was true, and it was good: you could hardly work up a decent argument over such a statement. George Washington himself had called religion and morality the "indispensable supports" of "political prosperity." "Our Constitution," affirmed John Adams, "was made only for a moral and religious people. It is wholly inadequate to the government of any other."

Religion, morality; morality, religion. The best thought of the day treated the two as inseparable companions on the national journey.

Not that the thinkers themselves were given to inquiring, with theological delicacy, into the exact and specific meaning of the word "religion." There were in America various species of Christianity.

The job of the federal government was not (as in the Mother Country, Britain) to choose among them and then promote as endlessly valid and valuable the religion of choice. That decision belonged to each citizen. Once the citizen had chosen, the right was his fully to effect that choice.

So matters continued until the last third of the 20th century, when the U.S. Supreme Court took upon itself to rewrite the tradition. Religion, owing to the new interpretation, became less an official blessing than a social irritant and a political danger. We had to corral it, the court said and kept on saying, whenever religion poked its head up in a place belonging to the taxpayers. To do otherwise would be to violate the rights of a constituency the founding fathers had not foreseen — the irreligious; those coolly indifferent to religion, if not hotly opposed to it.

There had, of course, been such as these from the beginning of time. But no Supreme Court had thought of elevating their distinctly minority preference to equality with the majority's historic conviction that an unseen God had endowed us with life and liberty.

In a sadly despiritualized time, the ***truth*** of religion came in for active criticism: often by clergymen nominally committed to advancing religious truth. As man thought more about man, and man's possibilities, he pondered less and less on God. Religion, by attrition of viewpoint, declined from truth to rarefied opinion. No responsible democratic government could give preference to one opinion over another, could it? The founding fathers must have spun round and round in their notably marked and well-visited graves.

One founding father — absent from the Philadelphia convention while on official business in France — left a unique testament to the value of religious conviction. He was Thomas Jefferson, a man associated by historians with free-thinking, rational inquiry, and like impulses of the Enlightenment. Jefferson was not the man to ratify truths he had not validated personally. Nor had he any use for "priests," as he called clergymen in general. These he blamed for corrupting "the simple religion of Jesus." Yet in that religion — as he identified it — he believed with intensity. Jefferson admired "innocence of (Jesus') character, the purity and sublimity of his moral precepts, the eloquence of his inculcations, the beauty of apologues in which he conveys them." "I am a real *Christian*," he wrote, "that is to say, a disciple of the doctrines of Jesus," as contrasted with doctrines Jefferson thought the "Platonists," led by St. Paul, had substituted for the original vision.

To gratify his own intuition that Jesus was a moralist, Jefferson pasted together this book: "The Life and Morals of Jesus of Nazareth." This occurred about 1819. Jefferson apparently undertook the project (as he undertook so much else) for his personal satisfaction and with no design of publishing it. The United States National Museum acquired the work in 1895, and in 1904 a congressional appropriation, sponsored by an Iowa congressman, John F. Lacey, secured its publication. For half a century afterwards, private groups presented a new "Life and Morals" to each newly elected member of Congress. The present reprinting revives that long-neglected practice.

Jefferson's book sounds very much like the Bible. It is the Bible, altered to remove, as Jefferson saw it, supernatural accretions that undermine Jesus' moral witness.

Jefferson pasted together those scriptural passages — in Greek, Latin, French, and English — that made up what he called "a paradigm of (Jesus') doctrines." "A more beautiful or precious morsel of ethics I have never seen," the former president said. In the Jeffersonian version, no angelic host heralds the birth in Bethlehem; no wise men bring gifts by the light of a star. There is no transfiguration on the mountain top, no institution of the Eucharist, no rending of the temple veil from top to bottom, no resurrection, and — for obvious reasons — no ascension. (Almost inexplicably, the Last Judgment is here, complete with "all the holy angels.") We see the stone rolled in place before the tomb. That is it: the story done, the witnesses dispersed.

Yet for page after page, up until that point, a marvel of instruction takes place: "Judge not, that ye be not judged . . ." "A good man, out of the treasure of the heart, bringeth forth good things: and an evil man, out of the evil treasure, bringeth forth evil things." "Verily I say unto you, Inasmuch as ye have done it unto one of the least of these my brethren, ye have done it unto me."

The priests could take care of what interested priests. Jesus' teaching, not his spiritual bona fides, was what interested Jefferson — the lofty standard of profession and practice to which he beckoned his hearers. It is no unique view in modern history: far less unique in our secular age than in Jefferson's time. But it is interesting to see what Jefferson made of all this. "The varieties in structure and action of the human mind as in those of the body," he wrote in 1809, "are the work of our Creator, against which it cannot be a religious duty to erect the standard of uniformity. *The practice of morality being necessary for the well-being of society* (italics mine), he has taken care to impress its precepts so indelibly on our hearts that they shall not be effaced by the subtleties of our brain. We all agree in the obligation of the moral precepts of Jesus."

There was a natural law, in other words. It had been written upon our hearts by "the Creator" (in that curious Enlightenment formulation). Jesus impressed it on us verbally. And here, as Jefferson compiled them, were his words.

Those who press the case against the intrusion of religion in public life normally cite Jefferson as a patron. His famous observation about the wall of separation between church and state is Exhibit A in the secularist case. That Jefferson vehemently opposed the intertwining of church and state is not in dispute. But the wall of separation is architecturally interesting only if we see the problem as being one of keeping church and state apart from each other. The truth is, scarcely anyone disagrees with that necessity. Hardly anyone wants a state church, a state-written creed, and so on. This is what logicians call the false dichotomy. The true dichotomy is between those who would keep Jesus' moral teachings out of public view on the basis of his religious connections and those who see no way of inculcating morality *without* introducing religion, broadly construed, into the national conversation. It is not too much for the latter to claim Thomas Jefferson as an ally.

How futile to argue about what Jefferson would have said concerning prayers at commencement and football games; about student-led vs. teacher-led prayer; about moments of silence and the use of public school facilities by religious groups. Jefferson is not here to ask. We have to reason it out by ourselves. But in doing so, it is hard not to note Jefferson's ringing endorsement of the moral principles of Jesus. What is the purpose after all of acknowledging God in a commencement exercise? It can only be to underscore the proper connection between religion and right behavior — that connection to which the founding fathers, including Jefferson, pointed with approval.

Those who deny any such connection are free to deny it. For that matter they are free to insist that gods are a paranoid figment of the primitive imagination: the sooner forgotten, the better for us all. Such happens not to be the American tradition. That tradition is one of abiding respect for religion as the underpinning of our manners and mores — both of which, the last time I looked, could stand drastic improvement.

Idiosyncratic as Jefferson's theology may have been, this book instructs us in the enduring worth of teachings that could not today — supposedly on Jefferson's intellectual authority! — be mentioned in a public school classroom.

The great curiosity here is that the Jesus of Jefferson is no conventional "religious" figure who imposes on his hearers a complicated and socially divisive creed. There are no creeds in the Jefferson Bible, and not a great deal of spirituality. There is only moral teaching — right and wrong, duty and obligation, freedom and service. To pick a constitutional fight with this Jesus requires an anti-religiosity intense, passionate, and, until today, wholly alien to the American Spirit.

Jefferson, thou shouldst be living at this hour! In any case, here is "The Life and Morals of Jesus of Nazareth" to broaden our perspective and deepen our insights into a controversy whose outcome is of the highest, the utmost urgency.

– *William Murchison*
Senior columnist, Dallas Morning News
Columnist, Creators Syndicate
Author: Reclaiming America's Morality
August 1996

PREFACE

by Judd W. Patton

When I first discovered the so-called "Jefferson Bible" in Bellevue University's Freeman Library, I was ecstatic. Here, in a very concise 82 pages, were the laws of "Nature's God" as compiled by Thomas Jefferson. I could imagine his own excitement at compiling the "most sublime edifice and benevolent code of morals which had ever been offered to man."

Let's place Jefferson's work into its proper context.

When Thomas Jefferson penned the eight-word phrase, "The Laws of Nature and of Nature's God" in the Declaration of Independence, he was not being poetic. These immortal eight words had a definite meaning. The phrase captured and expressed the value system for a new nation: the United States of America. Eleven years later our Founders established the necessary "by-laws"—"in Order to form a more perfect Union" and to "secure The Blessings of Liberty to ourselves and our Posterity."

In 1747, Ben Franklin wrote about the "great command of nature and nature's God." But it was three of the men most influential on America's Founding Fathers—Baron Charles Montesquieu (1689–1755), Sir William Blackstone (1723–1780), and John Locke (1632–1704)—who expounded on the meaning of the phrase.

In brief, these philosophers and legal authorities taught that natural law consists of two components: (1) the physical laws of nature discoverable by reason, and (2) the revealed laws of the Bible. Blackstone stated it plainly: "Upon these two foundations, the law of nature and the law of revelation, depend all human laws; that is to say, no human law should be suffered to contradict these."

Thomas Jefferson believed in the Creator God as the author of these natural and moral laws. Most significantly, he perceived that the long run survival of our American republic, this American experiment in self-government, required leaders and citizens who governed their lives by these precepts—"the Laws of Nature and of Nature's God."

Jefferson's "Bible" was the product of Jefferson's effort to compile these moral principles, the laws of "Nature's God." It was his expression of Christian morality, not his expression of Christian theology. It is in this context and spirit that our new edition of ***The Life and Morals of Jesus of Nazareth*** is reprinted and offered to all Americans.

Our re-publication could well be labeled a red-letter, study-bible edition of Jefferson's "Bible." It contains a summary in the margin that captures the story flow and highlights many moral precepts. For the serious student, it contains indexes of Scriptures, Parables, and Moral Principles. History enthusiasts will appreciate the appendices, which reveal the fascinating story of the discovery, debate, and controversy that surrounded the 1904 Congressional publication of Jefferson's work. Moreover, our Foreword and Introduction clear up the historic confusion over Jefferson's original intentions in producing the ***Philosophy of Jesus*** in 1804 and the ***Life and Morals of Jesus of Nazareth*** in 1820.

The reader will notice that no attempt was made to modernize the punctuation or spelling. Jefferson cut and pasted scriptures from a 1790s King James Version Bible. His page 1 is our page 1, etc. Our reproduction is exact, except for the removal of the Greek, Latin, and French columns that parallel the English texts.

When Congress published 3,000 copies of Jefferson's "Bible" for the use of the Senate and 6,000 copies for the use of the House in 1904, there were 90 Senators and 391 Representatives. That meant a distribution of 33 copies to each Senator and 15 copies to each Representative. Our distribution will be one copy to each member of Congress. It is our earnest hope that our leaders will study Jefferson's "Bible," in the tradition of Jefferson, and recapture America's fundamental value system as established in the Declaration of Independence—"the Laws of Nature and of Nature's God."

I wish to acknowledge many associates and colleagues without whom this reprint and distribution to members of Congress would never have become a reality. A special debt of gratitude and thanks go to Mark Beliles for his scholarly insights and additions to the Introduction; to Patricia Patterson for her help in locating biographical material and an appropriate photograph of John F. Lacey; to Image Building Communications – Jon Brooks for the cover design and Bridget Weide for keystroking the entire manuscript; to William Murchison for his stage-setting Foreword; to the Constitutional Heritage Institute, the Nebraska Christian Coalition, and Wallbuilders, Inc., for their sponsorship of the project; and to those American patriots for giving their support and written endorsements for the new edition of ***The Life and Morals of Jesus of Nazareth.***

– *Judd W. Patton*
Associate Professor of Economics
Bellevue University
Bellevue, Nebraska
August 1996

INTRODUCTION
JEFFERSON'S QUEST FOR PURE CHRISTIANITY AND GOOD GOVERNMENT

Thomas Jefferson (1743–1826)—third President of the United States, author of the Declaration of Independence, founder of the University of Virginia, and author of the Statutes for Religious Freedom in Virginia—produced two relatively unknown yet insightful works on morality: *The Philosophy of Jesus of Nazareth* in 1804 and *The Life and Morals of Jesus of Nazareth* in 1820.

The story and historical origins of these books are intriguing and notably relevant for our nation today.

The first version in 1804 had a different primary purpose from his later version. The purpose of the earlier version is apparent in its complete title: *The Philosophy of Jesus of Nazareth extracted from the account of his life and doctrines given by Matthew, Mark, Luke and John; Being an abridgement of the New Testament for the use of the Indians unembarrassed with matters of fact or faith beyond the level of their comprehensions.* The fact that this first version was originally "for the use of the Indians" is almost always overlooked by most commentators today.

On April 26, 1802, Jefferson signed into law the Act of Congress that funded the Society of the United Brethren "for Propagating the Gospel Among the Heathen" in the Northwest territory. This Act, which used federal dollars for the support of churches, clergy and missionary teachers' salaries, and Christian schools, was signed and approved again by Jefferson in March of 1803 and 1804. In October 1803, Jefferson submitted to the U.S. Senate his plan to purchase the Louisiana Territory and thus double the size of the United States. That same month, he also submitted the first of three treaties with Indian tribes living in the territory that again included federal money for paying salaries of missionaries and clergymen, but also for constructing churches for the Indians.[1]

In this light, Jefferson's motivations for making his first abridgement of the Gospels come more clearly into focus. In the few months following these treaties, he took the time while in the White House to cut out from two New Testaments the teachings and sayings of Jesus Christ. Henry Randall's biography of Jefferson states that he "conferred with friends on the expediency of having it published in the different Indian dialects as the most appropriate book for the Indians to be instructed to read in."[2] Jefferson felt that a smaller book would more easily translate into the multitude of Indian dialects, and could be printed in larger quantities than whole Bibles, which a number of clergymen and laymen had already been requesting him to support."[3] Thus we see the motivation for making his abridgement was primarily for teaching purposes in the Christian schools on the frontier. In 1803, prior to writing his abridgement,

Jefferson wrote a *Syllabus of the Merits of the Doctrines of Jesus* that he sent to Joseph Priestly. Jefferson urged Priestly to make "a digest of his (Christ's) moral doctrines, extracted in his own words from the Evangelists, and leaving out everything relative to his personal history and character." This was an explanation for what would be included in Jefferson's first abridgement: the teachings of Jesus only.

Interestingly, the *Philosophy of Jesus* has never been found! What has survived is a copy of the front page, a table of Scriptures and two New Testaments from which he clipped out the verses for his work. It was thus possible for historian Dickinson W. Adams to reconstruct Jefferson's *Philosophy of Jesus ... for the use of the Indians.* He did so in 1983 and it shows that, unlike Jefferson's later version, it still retained a few miracles such as the healing on the Sabbath in Luke 14:1-6 and the commission of Jesus to His disciples in Matthew 10 to go and heal the sick and raise the dead.[4] It includes Jesus' teaching about the resurrection of the dead, about His own second coming, about His role as judge of all men at the end of time, and about His place as son of God and Lord of a heavenly kingdom. He is also shown forgiving the sins of men and women in a manner reserved for God alone. These passages were retained by Jefferson because they related significantly to Jesus' teaching.

Nothing ever came about from Jefferson's project for the Indians; however, in 1816 Jefferson wrote to Charles Thomson: "I, too, have made a wee little book . . . which I call the *Philosophy of Jesus;* it is a paradigma of his doctrines, made by cutting the texts out of the book [the Bible], and arranging them on the pages of a blank book, in a certain order of time or subject." In the same letter, Jefferson added, "If I had time I would add to my little book the Greek, Latin and French texts in columns side by side."

Jefferson was unable to find that time until the winter of 1819–1820. He then revised and expanded his original, forty-six page compilation to what was eventually dubbed the "Jefferson Bible" by later commentators. His primary motive for this second version was no longer for the Indians but for his own personal study of the transcendent morality taught by Jesus. His letters from about 1813 to the end of his life in 1826 show a belief that the Bible had been corrupted over time and that "primitive Christianity" and the original teachings of Christ needed to be restored. This theme had been expressed earlier in the writings of Unitarians such as Joseph Priestly and of other "rational Christians" in New England, but in the Central Virginia Piedmont and other southern and western areas it had been popularized by the newer evangelical "Restoration" or primitive movement. These newer anti-creedal, anti-Calvinist, and anti-clerical movements, Jefferson identified as "the religionists calling themselves Christians."[5] Two of the four main leaders of the Restoration movement, Barton W. Stone and Alexander Campbell, were even anti-Trinitarian in theology. As historian Edwin Gaustad noted, Jefferson's statements about this time have "language remarkably like that of Campbell" although it is not known if they ever met.[6] Unfortunately, all those who have published the *Jefferson Bible* since 1903 have been almost universally either Unitarian or rationalist and secular in their approach, and their introductions to the book have left out the missionary motivation behind the first version or the evangelical "Restoration" movement's equally important source of influence in Jefferson's life. This has somewhat misrepresented Jefferson's motivations and beliefs to conform to their own theological assumptions or agendas.

Some have asserted that Jefferson was skeptical of the rest of the Bible, but it is important to note that, at the same time Jefferson was working on his abridgement, he also gave money to a Bible Society of Virginia in 1814 so that it could distribute whole Bibles to families in the state. He wrote to Samuel Greenhow: "I had not supposed there was a family in this State not possessing a Bible...I, therefore, enclose you cheerfully, an order...for fifty dollars, for the purposes of the Society."[7]

It would be more accurate to say that Jefferson's desire for his final abridgement of the Gospels was simply due to his admiration for and desire to focus upon the teachings of Jesus. This desire predated the popularity of later editions of Bibles which had the words of Christ printed in red for this same purpose. Jefferson, perhaps more than any other other American President, studied these words regularly and devotedly every night before retiring to bed.

Jefferson's "Bible," *The Life and Morals of Jesus of Nazareth,* remained hidden in Jefferson's family until it was discovered by Cyrus Adler, Librarian of the U.S. National Museum (now the Smithsonian) in 1886. Through his persistent efforts, Adler purchased it for the National Museum in 1895 for $400. Five years later, Representative John F. Lacey of Iowa made his own serendipitous discovery of Jefferson's work. He was so inspired by the book that he wrote a newspaper article about it that was widely reprinted throughout the country (See Appendix II). Most importantly, Lacey sponsored a Congressional Resolution in January, 1902, to publish 9,000 copies of "Jefferson's Morals of Jesus of Nazareth" at government expense for the *use* of our Senators and Representatives (See Appendix III for the actual Resolution and the Congressional discussion and debate about it).

But the story does not end there! After Congress published and distributed the 9,000 copies in 1904, a tradition began—by what group or groups is still unknown—of presenting a copy of Jefferson's work to our U.S. Senators and Representatives at their swearing in ceremonies with each new Congress. Anecdotal evidence indicates this custom continued for at least fifty years. Two former Nebraska Senators, Roman Hruska and Carl Curtis, still have their own copies. F. Forrester Church, in the Preface to a 1989 edition of "The Jefferson Bible" tells of his excitement when "In 1956, my father, Frank Church, won election to the United States Senate. As had been the custom since 1904, on the day of his swearing in he was presented with a copy of Thomas

Jefferson's Bible, *The Life and Morals of Jesus of Nazareth.* Two years later he gave the book to me."

This bygone, fifty-year tradition is re-established with the publication of the present, new edition of Jefferson's "Bible"—the most user-friendly edition ever!

The sponsors of this tradition —the Americanism Foundation, the Constitutional Heritage Institute, the Nebraska Christian Coalition, the Providence Foundation, and WallBuilders, Inc.—believe it is a most auspicious time to re-introduce Jefferson's work to our leaders and our nation. Many, if not most, of our national leaders recognize the moral decline that underlies—as the root cause of—our social, economic, and political evils. It is time to fully address this issue and begin the process of restoring and reclaiming our moral bearings and moral heritage. Thomas Jefferson's book can be the catalyst and inspiration for renewing America's heritage.

Thomas Jefferson clearly grasped the importance of a moral society for a society of free people. So, too, did most Americans over the decades, like many today. Consider the observations of Alexis de Tocqueville, that well-known historian and social philosopher, in his 1835 and 1840 work *Democracy in America:* "Religion in America . . . must be regarded as the foremost of the political institutions of that country; for if it does not impart a taste for freedom, it facilitates the use of it . . . I do not know whether all Americans have a sincere faith in their religion . . . But I am certain that they hold it to be indispensable to the maintenance of republican institutions. This opinion is not peculiar to a class of citizens or a party, but it belongs to the whole nation and to every rank of society."

Thomas Jefferson could have written these words! It was his belief in the synergistic relationship between morality and republican government that helped motivate him to search for religious truth and moral principles—culminating in his two works. As Governor of Virginia in 1779, he proclaimed a *"day of publick and solemn Thanksgiving and prayer to Almighty God,"* urging people to pray for God to "...establish the independence of these United States upon the basis of religion and virtue." Jefferson's proclamation closes by "recommending to all the good people of this commonwealth, to set apart the said day for those purposes..."[8] Then, in 1781, he expressed his belief that the liberties of a nation cannot "be thought secure when we have removed their only firm basis, a conviction in the minds of the people that these liberties are the gift of God."[9] And finally, as Jefferson began his Presidency in 1801, he declared, "The Christian religion, when . . . brought to the original purity and simplicity of its benevolent institutor, is a religion of all others most friendly to liberty, science, and the freest expansion of the human mind."

Jefferson found and published that simple and pure morality—*The Life and Morals of Jesus of Nazareth.* He said he found, "the most sublime and benevolent code of morals which has ever been offered to man." This code dealt with the heart of man and thereby "purified the waters at the fountain head," something no other philosopher or religions had ever done.

Jefferson's so-called "Bible" is one of his legacies to our nation—though relatively unknown. It reveals the moral precepts that are essential character traits for a free society and good government in America. Jefferson would agree with de Tocqueville: "America is great because America is good, and if America ever ceases to be good, America will cease to be great."

Representative John Lacey and members of Congress grasped Jefferson's vision when they decided in 1902 to publish his work. Representative Joel Heatwole of Minnesota, in a newspaper interview, said, "The excuse for printing it now is that the government has printed all the works of Thomas Jefferson, except this one." In the same interview, he revealed the real intent: "The object of having it printed was to lay the book open to the world, where it can do nothing but good." (See Appendix IV.)

The members of Congress passed Concurrent Resolution 15, after denying a resolution to rescind it, in 1902. By 1904 the Government printing office had produced "3,000 copies for the use of the Senate and 6,000 copies for the use of the House."

The *Life and Morals of Jesus of Nazareth* is rich with symbolism and substance. It is symbolic of the truth that neither Jefferson nor our forefathers wanted a "separation of religion and public life," but wanted a wall to protect religious expression and denominations *from* arbitrary government interference (The First Amendment). But the Jefferson "Bible" substance is infinitely greater. It contains the essence of Christian morality, approximately fifty precepts of "pure, genuine" morality as identified by the "man of the Millennium," according to George Will.

It is altogether fitting that our leaders be given the Jefferson "Bible" for their perusal and study. May they experience the words of Benjamin Franklin: "Whoever shall introduce into public affairs the principles of primitive Christianity will change the face of the world."

For those who would like an in-depth historical account of Jefferson's religious views and a detailed explanation of the origins of his two works, the following articles and books are highly recommended: (1) Cyrus Adler's "Introduction" to the 1904 edition of Jefferson's "Bible" (Appendix VI), (2) *Thomas Jefferson's Abridgement of the Words of Jesus of Nazareth* by Mark A. Beliles, 1993, (3) *Jeffersons' Extracts from the Gospels* by Dickenson W. Adams, Princeton University Press, 1983, and (4) *Christianity and the Constitution* by John Eidsmoe, Baker Books, 1987.

END NOTES

1. Robert L. Cord. ***Separation of Church and State: Historical Fact and Current Fiction.*** (New York, NY: Lambeth Press, 1982), pp. 241–270.
2. Henry S. Randall. ***The Life of Thomas Jefferson, 3 Vols.*** (New York, NY: Derby and Jackson, 1858). Vol. 3, p. 452.
3. See letters from Rev. Samuel Miller to Jefferson, 4 March, 1800, and from Edward Dowse to Jefferson, 3 April, 1803.
4. Dickinson W. Adams. ***Jefferson's Extracts From the Gospels.*** (Princeton, NJ: Princeton University Press, 1983). One other passage that Jefferson apparently used in this first version but which Adams left out quite arbitrarily was Matthew 11:2-9 where Jesus tells John the Baptist that His miracles authenticate His claim to be the Messiah.
5. Jefferson to Thomas Whittemore, 5 June, 1822.
6. Edwin Gaustad. ***Sworn On the Altar of God: A Religious Biography of Thomas Jefferson.*** (Grand Rapids, MI: W.B. Eerdmans Publishers, 1996), p. 145.
7. Jefferson to Samuel Greenhow, 31 January, 1814.
8. Jefferson's Proclamation for a Public Day of Thanksgiving and Prayer, 11 November, 1779.
9. Jefferson's ***Notes On the State of Virginia,*** 1781.

JEFFERSON'S TITLE PAGE

The

Life and Morals

of

Jesus of Nazareth

Extracted textually

from the Gospels

in

Greek, Latin

French & English.

JEFFERSON'S ORIGINAL TABLE OF CONTENTS

A Table
of the Texts ~~of this Extract~~ employed in this Narrative from the Evangelists, and of the order of their arrangement.

34. L. 10. 1–8. 10–12. mission of the LXX.
35. J. 7. 2–16. 19–26. 32. 43–53. the feast of the tabernacles.
36. J. 8. 1–11. the woman taken in Adultery.
37. J. 9. 1. 2. 3. to be born blind no proof of sin.
J. 10. 1–5. 11.–14. 16. the good shepherd.
38. L. 10. 25–37. love god & thy neighbor. parable of the Samaritan.
39. L. 11. 1–13. form of prayer.
40. L. 14. 1–6. the Sabbath.
41. 7–24. the bidden to a feast.
42. 28–32. precepts.
3.44. L. 15. 1–32. parables of the lost sheep and Prodigal son.
45. L. 16. 1–15. parable of the unjust steward.
46. 18–31. parable of Lazarus.
48. L. 17. 1–4. 7–10. 20. 26–36. precepts to be always ready.
49. L. 18. 1–14. parables of the widow & judge, the Pharisee & Publican.
0.51. L. 10. 38–42. Mt. 19. 1–26. precepts.
52. Mt. 20. 1–16. parable of the laborers in the vineyard.
54. L. 19. 1–28. Zaccheus, & the parable of the talents.
6. Mt. 21. 1–3. 6–8. 10. J. 12. 19–24. Mt. 21. 17. goes to Jerusalem & Bethany.
Mk. 11. 12. 15–19. the traders cast out from the temple.
Mk. 11. 27. Mt. 21. 27–31. parable of the two sons.
7. Mt. 21. 33. Mk. 12. 1–9. ^Mt. 21. 45. 46. parable of the vineyard & husbandmen.
8. Mt. 22. 1.–14. parable of the king and wedding.
59. 15–33. tribute. marriage. resurrection.
60. Mk. 12. 28–31. Mt. 22. 40. Mk. 12. 32. 33. the two commandments.
62. Mt. 23. 1–33. precepts. pride. hypocrisy. swearing.
3. Mk. 12. 41–44. the widow's mite.
4. Mt. 24. 1. 2. 16–21. 32. 33. 36–39. 40.–44. Jerusalem & the day of judgment.
45–51. the faithful and wise servant.
65. Mt. 25. 1–13. parable of the ten virgins.
66. 14–30. parable of the talents.
68. L. 21. 34–36. Mt. 25. 31–46. the day of judgment.
69. Mk. 14. 1–8. a woman anointeth him.

	Mt. 26. 14–16. Judas undertakes to point out Jesus.
70.71.	17–20. L. 22. 24–27. J. 13. 2. 4–17. 21–26. 31. 34. 35. Mt. 26. 31. 33.
72.	L. 22. 33–34. Mt. 26. 35–45. precepts to his desciples, washes their feet, trouble of mind and prayer.
73.	J. 18. 1–3. Mt. 26. 48–50. Judas conducts the officers to Jesus.
74.	J. 18. 4–8. Mt. 26. 50–52. 55. 56. Mk. 14. 51. 52. Mt. 26. 57. J. 18. 15. 16. 18. 17
75.	J. 18. 25. 26. 27. Mt. 26. 75. J. 18. 19–23. Mk. 14. 55–61. L. 22. 67. 68. 70. Mk. 14. 63–65. he is arrested & carried before Caiaphas the High priest & is condemned.
76.	J. 18. 28–31. 33–38. L. 23. 5. Mt. 27. 13. is then carried to Pilate.
77.	L. 23. 6–12. who sends him to Herod.
78.	L. 23. 13–16. Mt. 27. 15–23. 26. recieves him back, scourges and delivers him to execution.
79. 80. 81.	Mt. 27. 27. 29–31. 3–8. L. 23. 26–32. J. 19. 17–24. Mt. 27. 39–43. L. 23. 39–41. 34. J. 19. 25–27. Mt. 27. 46–50. 55. 56. his crucifixion, death and burial.
.	J. 19. 31–34. 38–42. Mt. 27. 60. his burial.

LUKE 2:
1-7

AND it came to pass in those days, that there went out a decree from Cesar Augustus, that all the world should be taxed.
2 *(And* this taxing was first made when Cyrenius was governor of Syria.)
3 And all went to be taxed, every one into his own city.
4 And Joseph also went up from Galilee, out of the city of Nazareth, into Judea, unto the city of David, which is called Bethlehem (because he was of the house and lineage of David,)
5 To be taxed with Mary his espoused wife, being great with child.
6 And so it was, that, while they were there, the days were accomplished that she should be delivered.
7 And she brought forth her firstborn son, and wrapped him in swaddling-clothes, and laid him in a manger; because there was no room for them in the inn.

Joseph and Mary go to Bethlehem, where Jesus is born.

LUKE 2:
21, 39

21 And when eight days were accomplished for the circumcising of the child, his name was called JESUS,
39 And when they had perfomed all things according to the law of the Lord, they returned into Galilee, to their own city Nazareth.

He is circumcised and named. They return to Nazareth.

LUKE 2:
40, 42-45

40 And the child grew, and waxed strong in spirit, filled with wisdom;
42 And when he was twelve years old, they went up to Jerusalem, after the custom of the feast.
43 And when they had fulfilled the days, as they returned, the child Jesus tarried behind in Jerusalem; and Joseph and his mother knew not *of it.*
44 But they supposing him to have been in the company, went a day's journey; and they sought him among *their* kinsfolk and acquaintance.
45 And when they found him not, they turned back again to Jerusalem, seeking him.

At 12 years of age, He accompanies His parents to the Passover at Jerusalem.

LUKE 2: 46-48, 51, 52	46 And it came to pass, that after three days they found him in the temple, sitting in the midst of the doctors, both hearing them, and asking them questions. 47 And all that heard him were astonished at his understanding and answers. 48 And when they saw him, they were amazed: and his mother said unto him, Son, why hast thou thus dealt with us? behold, thy father and I have sought thee sorrowing. 51 And he went down with them, and came to Nazareth, and was subject unto them: 52 And Jesus increased in wisdom and stature.	*Jesus amazes the scholars.*
LUKE 3: 1, 2	NOW in the fifteenth year of the reign of Tiberius Cesar, Pontius Pilate being governor of Judea, and Herod being tetrarch of Galilee, and his brother Philip tetrarch of Iturea and of the region of Trachonitus, and Lysanias the tetrarch of Abilene, 2 Annas and Caiaphas being the high priests,	*John baptizes in the Jordan River.*
MARK 1: 4	4 John did baptize in the wilderness,	
MATT. 3: 4-6	4 And the same John had his raiment of camels' hair, and a leathern girdle about his loins; and his meat was locusts and wild honey. 5 Then went out to him Jerusalem, and all Judea, and all the region round about Jordan. 6 And were baptized of him in Jordan,	
MATT. 3: 13	13 Then cometh Jesus from Galilee to Jordan unto John, to be baptized of him.	*Jesus is baptized at 30 years of age.*
LUKE 3: 23	23 And Jesus himself began to be about thirty years of age,	
JOHN 2: 12	12 After this he went down to Capernaum, he, and his mother, and his brethren, and his disciples; and they continued there not many days.	

JOHN 2: 13-16

Jesus drives the traders out of the temple.

13 And the Jews' passover was at hand; and Jesus went up to Jerusalem,
14 And found in the temple those that sold oxen, and sheep, and doves, and the changers of money, sitting:
15 And, when he had made a scourge of small cords, he drove them all out of the temple, and the sheep, and the oxen; and poured out the changers' money, and overthrew the tables;
16 And said unto them that sold doves, Take these things hence; make not my Father's house an house of merchandise.

JOHN 3: 22

He baptizes but retires unto Galilee on the death of John the Baptist.

22 After these things came Jesus and his disciples into the land of Judea; and there he tarried with them, and baptized.

MATT 4:12

12 Now, when Jesus had heard that John was cast into prison, he departed into Galilee:

MARK 6: 17-23

17 For Herod himself had sent forth, and laid hold upon John, and bound him in prison for Herodias' sake, his brother Philip's wife; for he had married her.
18 For John had said unto Herod, It is not lawful for thee to have thy brother's wife.
19 Therefore Herodias had a quarrel against him, and would have killed him; but she could not.
20 For Herod feared John, knowing that he was a just man, and an holy, and observed him; and when he heard him, he did many things, and heard him gladly.
21 And when a convenient day was come, that Herod, on his birthday, made a supper to his lords, high captains, and chief *estates* of Galilee;
22 And when the daughter of the said Herodias came in and danced, and pleased Herod, and them that sat with him, the king said unto the damsel, Ask of me whatsoever thou wilt, and I will give *it* thee.
23 And he sware unto her, Whatsoever thou shalt ask of me, I will give *it* thee, unto the half of my kingdom.

MARK 6: 24-28

24 And she went forth, and said unto her mother, What shall I ask? and she said, The head of John the Baptist.
25 And she came in straightway with haste unto the king, and asked, saying, I will that thou give me, by and by in a charger, the head of John the Baptist.
26 And the king was exceeding sorry; *yet* for his oath's sake, and for their sakes which sat with him, he would not reject her.
27 And immediately the king sent an executioner, and commanded his head to be brought: and he went and beheaded him in the prison;
28 And brought his head in a charger, and gave it to the damsel: and the damsel gave it to her mother.

MARK 1: 21, 22

Jesus teaches in the synagogue with authority.

21 And they went into Capernaum; and straightway on the sabbath-day, he entered into the synagogue, and taught.
22 And they were astonished at his doctrine: for he taught them as one that had authority, and not as the scribes.

MATT. 12: 1-5

Jesus explains the proper use of the Sabbath.

AT that time Jesus went on the sabbath-day through the corn; and his disciples were an hungered, and began to pluck the ears of corn, and to eat.
2 But when the Pharisees saw *it,* they said unto him, Behold, thy disciples do that which is not lawful to do upon the sabbath-day.
3 But he said unto them, Have ye not read what David did when he was an hungered, and they that were with him;
4 How he entered into the house of God, and did eat the shewbread, which was not lawful for him to eat, neither for them which were with him, but only for the priests?
5 Or, have ye not read in the law, how that on the sabbath-days the priests in the temple profane the sabbath, and are blameless?

MATT. 12: 9-12

9 And when he was departed thence, he went into their synagogue:

10 And, behold, there was a man which had *his* hand withered. And they asked him, saying, Is it lawful to heal on the sabbath-days? that they might accuse him.

11 And he said unto them, What man shall there be among you, that shall have one sheep, and if it fall into a pit on the sabbath-day, will he not lay hold on it, and lift *it* out?

12 How much then is a man better than a sheep? Wherefore it is lawful to do well on the sabbath-days.

MARK 2: 27

27 And he said unto them, The sabbath was made for man, and not man for the sabbath:

Sabbath Day made for mankind.

MATT. 12: 14, 15

14 Then the Pharisees went out, and held a council against him, how they might destroy him.

15 But when Jesus knew *it,* he withdrew himself from thence: and great multitudes followed him,

LUKE 6: 12-17

12 And it came to pass in those days, that he went up into a mountain to pray, and continued all night in prayer to God.

13 And when it was day, he called *unto him* his disciples; and of them he chose twelve, whom also he named Apostles;

14 Simon, (whom he also named Peter,) and Andrew his brother, James and John, Philip and Bartholomew,

15 Matthew and Thomas, James *the son* of Alpheus, and Simon called Zelotes,

16 And Judas *the brother* of James, and Judas Iscariot, which also was the traitor.

17 And he came down with them, and stood in the plain; and the company of his disciples, and a great multitude of people out of all Judea and Jerusalem, and from the sea-coast of Tyre and Sidon, which came to hear him,

Jesus calls His disciples: Peter, Andrew, James, John, Philip, Bartholomew, Matthew, Thomas, James, Simon, Judas, and Judas Iscariot.

MATT. 5: 1-12

The Sermon on the Mount.

AND seeing the multitudes, he went up into a mountain: and when he was set, his disciples came unto him:

2 And he opened his mouth, and taught them, saying,

The blessings, also known as the Beatitudes . . .

3 Blessed*are* the poor in spirit: for their's is the kingdom of heaven.

4. Blessed *are* they that mourn: for they shall be comforted.

5 Blessed *are* the meek: for they shall inherit the earth.

6 Blessed *are* they which do hunger and thirst after righteousness: for they shall be filled.

7 Blessed *are* the merciful: for they shall obtain mercy.

8 Blessed *are* the pure in heart: for they shall see God.

9 Blessed *are* the peace-makers: for they shall be called the children of God.

10 Blessed*are* they which are persecuted for righteousness' sake: for their's is the kingdom of heaven.

11 Blessed *are* ye when *men* shall revile you, and persecute *you,* and shall say all manner of evil against you falsely, for my sake.

12 Rejoice, and be exceeding glad; for great *is* your reward in heaven: for so persecuted they the prophets which were before you.

LUKE 6: 24-26

... and the woes.

24 But woe unto you that are rich! for ye have received your consolation.

25 Woe unto you that are full! for ye shall hunger. Woe unto you that laugh now! for ye shall mourn and weep.

26 Woe unto you when all men shall speak well of you! for so did their fathers to the false prophets.

MATT. 5: 13, 14

Believers are salt and light to the world.

13 Ye are the salt of the earth: but if the salt have lost his savour, wherewith shall it be salted: it is thenceforth good for nothing, but to be cast out, and to be trodden under foot of men.

14 Ye are the light of the world. A city that is set on an hill cannot be hid.

MATT. 5: 15-24

15 Neither do men light a candle, and put it under a bushel, but on a candlestick, and it giveth light unto all that are in the house.
16 Let your light so shine before men, that they may see your good works, and glorify your Father which is in heaven.
17 Think not that I am come to destroy the law, or the prophets: I am not come to destroy, but to fulfil.

Christ did not come to destroy the law but to fulfill and magnify it.

18 For verily I say unto you, Till heaven and earth pass, one jot or one tittle shall in no wise pass from the law, till all be fulfilled.
19 Whosoever, therefore, shall break one of these least commandments and shall teach men so, he shall be called the least in the kingdom of heaven: but whosoever shall do, and teach *them,* the same shall be called great in the kingdom of heaven.
20 For I say unto you, That except your righteousness shall exceed*the righteousness* of the scribes and Pharisees, ye shall in no case enter into the kingdom of heaven.
21 Ye have heard that it was said by them of old time, Thou shalt not kill; and, whosoever shall kill, shall be in danger of the judgment:

Murder begins in one's heart — the spirit of the law.

22 But I say unto you, That whosoever is angry with his brother without a cause, shall be in danger of the judgment: and whosoever shall say to his brother, Raca, shall be in danger of the council: but whosoever shall say, Thou fool, shall be in danger of hell fire.
23 Therefore, if thou bring thy gift to the altar, and there rememberest that thy brother hath aught against thee;
24 Leave there thy gift before the altar, and go thy way; first be reconciled to thy brother, and then come and offer thy gift.

MATT. 5: 25-35

25 Agree with thine adversary quickly, whilst thou art in the way with him; lest at any time the adversary deliver thee to the judge, and the judge deliver thee to the officer, and thou be cast into prison.

Strive to resolve conflict quickly.

26 Verily I say unto thee, Thou shalt by no means come out thence, till thou hast paid the uttermost farthing.

27 Ye have heard that it was said by them of old time, Thou shalt not commit adultery:

Adultery begins in the heart (mind).

28 But I say unto you, That whosoever looketh on a woman, to lust after her, hath committed adultery with her already in his heart.

29 And if thy right eye offend thee, pluck it out, and cast *it* from thee: for it is profitable for thee, that one of thy members should perish, and not *that* thy whole body should be cast into hell.

30 And if thy right hand offend thee, cut it off, and cast *it* from thee: for it is profitable for thee, that one of thy members should perish, and not *that* thy whole body should be cast into hell.

31 It hath been said, Whosoever shall put away his wife, let him give her a writing of divorcement:

Marriage is sacred and binding.

32 But I say unto you, That whosoever shall put away his wife, saving for the cause of fornication, causeth her to commit adultery: and whosoever shall marry her that is divorced, committeth adultery.

33 Again, ye have heard that it hath been said by them of old time, Thou shalt not forswear thyself, but shalt perform unto the Lord thine oaths:

Oaths forbidden.

34 But I say unto you, Swear not at all: neither by heaven, for it is God's throne:

35 Nor by the earth: for it is his

MATT. 5: 36-47

footstool: neither by Jerusalem; for it is the city of the great King:
36 Neither shalt thous swear by thy head; because thou canst not make one hair white or black.
37 But let your communication be, Yea, yea; Nay, nay: for whatsoever *is* more than these cometh of evil.

Let your yes be yes, and your no be no.

38 Ye have heard that it hath been said, An eye for an eye, and a tooth for a tooth:
39 But I say unto you, That ye resist not evil: but whosoever shall smite thee on thy right cheek, turn to him the other also.
40 And if any man will sue thee at the law, and take away thy coat, let him have *thy* cloak also.
41 And whosoever shall compel thee to go a mile, go with him twain.
42 Give to him that asketh thee; and from him that would borrow of thee, turn not thou away.

"Go the extra mile" when dealing with people.

43 Ye have heard that it hath been said, Thou shalt love thy neighbour, and hate thine enemy:
44 But I say unto you, Love your enemies, bless them that curse you, do good to them that hate you, and pray for them which despitefully use you, and persecute you;
45 That ye may be the children of your Father which is in heaven: for he maketh his sun to rise on the evil and on the good, and sendeth rain on the just and on the unjust.
46 For if ye love them which love you, what reward have ye? do not even the publicans the same?
47 And if ye salute your brethren only, what do ye more *than others?* do not even the publicans so?

Love and pray for your enemies.

LUKE 6: 34-36

Develop a merciful and giving way of life.

34 And if ye lend *to them* of whom ye hope to receive, what thank have ye? for sinners also lend to sinners, to receive as much again.

35 But love ye your enemies, and do good, and lend hoping for nothing again: and your reward shall be great, and ye shall be the children of the Highest: for he is kind unto the unthankful, and *to* the evil.

36 Be ye, therefore, merciful, as your Father also is merciful.

MATT. 6: 1-8

How to give to the needy: privately, without fanfare.

TAKE heed that ye do not your alms before men, to be seen of them: otherwise ye have no reward of your Father which is in heaven.

2 Therefore, when thou doest *thine* alms, do not sound a trumpet before thee, as the hypocrites do in the synogogues, and in the streets, that they may have glory of men. Verily I say unto you, They have their reward.

3 But when thou doest alms, let not thy left hand know what thy right hand doeth:

4 That thine alms may be in secret: and thy Father, which seeth in secret, himself shall reward thee openly.

How to pray: in secret without vain repetitions.

5 And when thou prayest, thou shalt not be as the hypocrites *are:* for they love to pray standing in the synagogues, and in the corners of the streets, that they may be seen of men. Verily I say unto you, They have their reward.

6 But thou, when thou prayest, enter into thy closet; and, when thou hast shut thy door, pray to thy Father which is in secret; and thy Father which seeth in secret, shall reward thee openly.

7 But when ye pray, use not vain repetitions, as the heathen *do:* for they think that they shall be heard for their much speaking.

8 Be not ye, therefore, like unto them: for your Father knoweth what things ye have need of, before ye ask him.

MATT. 6: 9-22

The Lord's "model" prayer.

9 After this manner, therefore, pray ye: Our Father which art in heaven; Hallowed be thy name.
10 Thy kingdom come. Thy will be done in earth, as *it is* in heaven.
11 Give us this day our daily bread.
12 And forgive us our debts, as we forgive our debtors.
13 And lead us not into temptation; but deliver us from evil: For thine is the kingdom, and the power, and the glory, for ever. Amen.
14 For if ye forgive men their trespasses, your heavenly Father will also forgive you:
15 But if ye forgive not men their trespasses, neither will your Father forgive your trespasses.

How to fast: others need not know.

16 Moreover, when ye fast, be not as the hypocrites, of a sad countenance: for they disfigure their faces, that they may appear unto men to fast. Verily I say unto you, They have their reward.
17 But thou, when thou fastest, anoint thine head, and wash thy face;
18 That thou appear not unto men to fast, but unto thy Father which is in secret: and thy Father, which seeth in secret, shall reward thee openly.

Lay up treasures in heaven.

19 Lay not up for yourselves treasures upon earth, where moth and rust doth corrupt, and where thieves break through and steal:
20 But lay up for yourselves treasures in heaven, where neither moth nor rust doth corrupt, and where thieves do not break through nor steal:
21 For where your treasure is, there will your heart be also.

The eye is the lamp of the body.

22 The light of the body is the eye: if, therefore, thine eye be single, thy whole body shall be full of light.

MATT. 6:
23-34

23 But if thine eye be evil, thy whole body shall be full of darkness. If, therefore, the light that is in thee be darkness, how great *is* that darkness?

An evil eye — selfishness, affects a person's whole life.

24 No man can serve two masters: for either he will hate the one, and love the other; or else he will hold to the one, and despise the other. Ye cannot serve God and mammon.

One cannot serve God and riches.

25 Therefore I say unto you, Take no thought for your life, what ye shall eat or what ye shall drink; nor yet for your body, what ye shall put on. Is not the life more than meat, and the body than raiment?

Do not worry unnecessarily about your physical life.

26 Behold the fowls of the air: for they sow not, neither do they reap, nor gather into barns; yet your heavenly Father feedeth them. Are ye not much better than they?

27 Which of you, by taking thought, can add one cubit unto his stature?

28 And why take ye thought for raiment? Consider the lilies of the field how they grow: they toil not, neither do they spin;

29 And yet I say unto you, That even Solomon in all his glory was not arrayed like one of these.

30 Wherefore, if God so clothe the grass of the field, which to day is, and to morrow is cast into the oven, *shall he* not much more *clothe* you? O ye of little faith;

31 Therefore, take no thought, saying, What shall we eat? or, What shall we drink? or, Wherewithal shall we be clothed?

32 (For after all these things do the Gentiles seek:) for your heavenly Father knoweth that ye have need of all these things.

33 But seek ye first the kingdom of God, and his righteousness; and all these things shall be added unto you.

Seek above all else the Kingdom of God.

34 Take therefore no thought for the morrow: for the morrow shall take thought for the things of itself. Sufficient unto the day *is* the evil thereof.

MATT. 7: 1-2	JUDGE not, that ye be not judged. 2 For with what judgment ye judge, ye shall be judged: and with what measure ye mete, it shall be measured to you again.	*Do not condemn others.*
LUKE 6: 38	38 Give, and it shall be given unto you; good measure, pressed down, and shaken together, and running over, shall men give into your bosom.	*Give – and one will be blessed.*
MATT. 7: 3-12	3 And why beholdest thou the mote that is in thy brother's eye, but considerest not the beam that is in thine own eye? 4 Or how wilt thou say to thy brother, Let me pull out the mote out of thine eye; and, behold, a beam *is* in thine own eye? 5 Thou hypocrite! first cast out the beam out of thine own eye; and then shalt thou see clearly to cast out the mote out thy brother's eye. 6 Give not that which is holy unto the dogs; neither cast ye your pearls before swine, lest they trample them under their feet, and turn again and rend you.	*Judge oneself. Don't be a hypocrite.*
	7 Ask, and it shall be given you; seek, and ye shall find; knock, and it shall be opened unto you: 8 For every one that asketh, receiveth; and he that seeketh, findeth; and to him that knocketh, it shall be opened. 9 Or what man is there of you, whom if his son ask bread, will he give him a stone? 10 Or if he ask a fish, will he give him a serpent? 11 If ye then, being evil, know how to give good gifts unto your children, how much more shall your Father, which is in heaven, give good things to them that ask him?	*Keep asking, seeking, and knocking for spiritual knowledge.*
	12 Therefore all things whatsoever ye would that men should do to you, do ye even so to them: for this is the law and the prophets.	*Golden Rule: Do to others as you would have them do to you.*

MATT. 7: 13-20

13 Enter ye in at the strait gate; for wide *is* the gate, and broad *is* the way, that leadeth to destruction, and many there be which go in thereat:

Choose the Way of life.

14 Because strait *is* the gate, and narrow *is* the way, which leadeth unto life, and few there be that find it.

15 Beware of false prophets, which come to you in sheep's clothing, but inwardly they are ravening wolves.

You will know people by their fruits.

16 Ye shall know them by their fruits. Do men gather grapes of thorns, or figs of thistles?

17 Even so, every good tree bringeth forth good fruit; but a corrupt tree bringeth forth evil fruit.

18 A good tree cannot bring forth evil fruit, neither *can* a corrupt tree bring forth good fruit.

19 Every tree that bringeth not forth good fruit is hewn down, and cast into the fire.

20 Wherefore by their fruits ye shall know them.

MATT. 12: 35-37

35 A good man, out of the good treasure of the heart, bringeth forth good things: and an evil man, out of the evil treasure, bringeth forth evil things.

36 But I say unto you, That every idle word that men shall speak, they shall give account thereof in the day of judgment.

God will hold men accountable for their words.

37 For by thy words thou shalt be justified, and by thy words thou shalt be condemned.

MATT. 7: 24, 25

24 Therefore whosoever heareth these sayings of mine, and doeth them, I will liken him unto a wise man, which built his house upon a rock:

Parable of Building on Rock, not Sand.

25 And the rain descended, and the floods came, and the winds blew, and beat upon that house; and it fell not: for it was founded upon a rock.

MATT. 7: 26-29	26 And every one that heareth these sayings of mine, and doeth them not, shall be likened unto a foolish man, which built his house upon the sand:	*Success is assured if one builds on Christ's principles.*
	27 And the rain descended, and the floods came, and the winds blew, and beat upon that house; and it fell, and great was the fall of it.	*Failure is assured if one ignores Christ's principles.*
	28 And it came to pass when Jesus had ended these sayings, the people were astonished at his doctrine:	
	29 For he taught them as *one* having authority, and not as the scribes.	
MATT. 8: 1	WHEN he was come down from the mountain, great multitudes followed him.	
MARK 6: 6	6 And he went round about the villages, teaching.	
MATT. 11: 28-30	28 Come unto me, all *ye* that labour and are heavy laden, and I will give you rest.	*Jesus gives true rest, not religious bondage.*
	29 Take my yoke upon you, and learn of me; for I am meek and lowly in heart: and ye shall find rest unto your souls.	
	30 For my yoke *is* easy, and my burden is light.	
LUKE 7: 36-38	36 And one of the Pharisees desired him that he would eat with him. And he went into the Pharisee's house, and sat down to meat.	*A woman anoints Him and is forgiven.*
	37 And, behold, a woman in the city, which was a sinner, when she knew that *Jesus* sat at meat in the Pharisee's house, brought an alabaster box of ointment,	
	38 And stood at his feet behind *him* weeping, and began to wash his feet with tears, and did wipe *them* with the hairs of her head, and kissed his feet, and anointed *them* with the ointment.	

LUKE 7: 39-46

39 Now, when the Pharisee which had bidden him saw *it,* he spake within himself, saying, This man, if he were a prophet, would have known who and what manner of woman *this is* that toucheth him; for she is a sinner.
40 And Jesus, answering, said unto him, Simon, I have somewhat to say unto thee. And he saith, Master, say on.

Parables of a Creditor Who Forgives Two Debtors.

41 There was a certain creditor, which had two debtors: the one owed five hundred pence, and the other fifty.
42 And when they had nothing to pay, he frankly forgave them both. Tell me, therefore, which of them will love him most?
43 Simon answered, and said, I suppose that *he* to whom he forgave most. And he said unto him, Thou hast rightly judged.
44 And he turned to the woman, and said unto Simon, Seest thou this woman? I entered into thine house, thou gavest me no water for my feet: but she hath washed my feet with tears, and wiped *them* with the hairs of her head.
45 Thou gavest me no kiss: but this woman, since the time I came in, hath not ceased to kiss my feet.
46 My head with oil thou didst not anoint: but this woman hath anointed my feet with ointment.

MARK 3: 31-35

Precepts:

31 There came then his brethren and his mother, and, standing without, sent unto him, calling him.
32 And the multitude sat about him, and they said unto him, Behold, thy mother and thy brethren without seek for thee.
33 And he answered them, saying, Who is my mother, or my brethren?

Doers of God's will are God's people.

34 And he looked round about on them which sat about him, and said, Behold my mother and my brethren!
35 For whosoever shall do the will of God, the same is my brother, and my sister, and mother.

LUKE 12: 1-7

IN the mean time, when there were gathered together an innumerable multitude of people, insomuch that they trode one upon another, he began to say unto his disciples first of all, Beware ye of the leaven of the Pharisees, which is hypocrisy.

Beware of hypocrisy.

2 For there is nothing covered, that shall not be revealed; neither hid, that shall not be known.

3 Therefore whatsoever ye have spoken in darkness, shall be heard in the light; and that which ye have spoken in the ear in closets, shall be proclaimed upon the house-tops.

4 And I say unto you, my friends, Be not afraid of them that kill the body, and after that have no more that they can do.

Fear (respect) God.

5 But I will forewarn you whom ye shall fear: Fear him, which, after he hath killed, hath power to cast into hell; yea, I say unto you, Fear him.

6 Are not five sparrows sold for two farthings? and not one of them is forgotten before God.

7 But even the very hairs of your head are an numbered. Fear not, therefore; ye are of more value than many sparrows.

LUKE 12: 13-15

13 And one of the company said unto him, Master, speak to my brother, that he divide the inheritance with me.

14 And he said unto him, Man, who made me a judge, or a divider over you?

15 And he said unto them, Take heed, and beware of covetousness; for a man's life consistence not in the abundance of the things which he possesseth.

Beware of covetousness.

LUKE 12: 16

16 And he spake a parable unto them, saying, The ground of a certain rich man brought forth plentifully.

Parable of the Rich Fool.

LUKE 12: 17-21	17 And he thought within himself, saying, What shall I do, because I have no room where to bestow my fruits? 18 And he said, This will I do: I will pull down my barns, and build greater; and there will I bestow all my fruits and my goods. 19 And I will say to my soul, Soul, thou hast much goods laid up for many years: take thine ease, eat, drink, *and* be merry. 20 But God said unto him, *Thou* fool! this night thy soul shall be required of thee; then whose shall those things be, which thou hast provided? 21 So *is* he that layeth up treasure for himself, and is not rich toward God.	***Don't be foolish, be rich toward God.***
LUKE 12: 22-30	**22 And he said unto his disciples,** Therefore I say unto you, Take no thought for your life, what ye shall eat; neither for the body, what ye shall put on. 23 The life is more than meat, and the body *is more* than raiment. 24 Consider the ravens: for they neither sow nor reap; which neither have storehouse nor barn; and God feedeth them: how much more are ye better than the fowls? 25 And which of you, with taking thought, can add to his stature one cubit? 26 If ye then be not able to do that thing which is least, why take ye thought for the rest? 27 Consider the lilies how they grow: they toil not, they spin not; and yet I say unto you, That Solomon, in all his glory, was not arrayed like one of these. 28 If then God so clothe the grass, which is to-day in the field, and to-morrow is cast into the oven; how much more *will he clothe* you? O ye of little faith! 29 And seek not ye what ye shall eat, or what ye shall drink; neither be ye of doubtful mind. 30 For all these things do the nations of the world seek after: and your Father knoweth that ye have need of these things.	***Precepts:*** ***Don't put undue emphasis on the physical things of life.***

LUKE 12:
31-43

31 But rather seek ye the kingdom of God; and all these things shall be added unto you.

Seek the Kingdom of God.

32 Fear not, little flock; for it is your Father's good pleasure to give you the kingdom.

God desires to give the Kingdom to His people.

33 Sell that ye have, and give alms; provide yourselves bags which wax not old, a treasure in the heavens that faileth not, where no thief approacheth, neither moth corrupteth.

34 For where your treasure is, there will your heart be also.

35 Let your loins be girded about, and your lights burning:

36 And ye yourselves like unto men that wait for their lord, when he will return from the wedding; that when he cometh and knocketh, they may open unto him immediately.

Parable of the Wise Stewards.

37 Blessed *are* those servants, whom the lord, when he cometh, shall find watching: verily I say unto you, That he shall gird himself, and make them to sit down to meat, and will come forth and serve them.

Watch for the return of Christ.

38 And if he shall come in the second watch, or come in the third watch, and find *them* so, blessed are the servants.

39 And this know, that if the good man of the house had known what hour the thief would come, he would have watched, and not have suffered his house to be broken through.

40 Be ye, therefore, ready also: for the Son of Man cometh at an hour when ye think not.

41 Then Peter said unto him, Lord, speakest thou this parable unto us, or even to all?

42 And the Lord said, Who then is that faithful and wise steward, whom *his* lord shall make ruler over his household, to give *them their* portion of meat in due season?

Always be a faithful and wise steward in this life. God will reward this person.

43 Blessed *is* that servant, whom his lord, when he cometh, shall find so doing.

LUKE 12:
44-48

44 Of a truth I say unto you, That he will make him ruler over all that he hath.

45 But, and if that servant say in his heart, My lord delayeth his coming; and shall begin to beat the men-servants, and maidens, and to eat and drink, and to be drunken;

46 The lord of that servant will come in a day when he looketh not for *him,* and at an hour when he is not aware, and will cut him in sunder,

47 And that servant, which knew his lord's will, and prepared not *himself,* neither did according to his will, shall be beaten with many *stripes.*

48 But he that knew not, and did commit things worthy of stripes, shall be beaten with few *stripes.* For unto whomsoever much is given, of him shall be much required: and to whom men have committed much, of him they will ask the more.

Much is required of the person who has been given much.

LUKE 12:
54-59

54 **he said also to the people,** When ye see a cloud rise out of the west, straightway ye say, There cometh a shower, and so it is.

55 And when *ye see* the south wind blow, ye say, There will be heat; and it cometh to pass.

56 Ye hypocrites! ye can discern the face of the sky and of the earth; but how is it, that ye do not discern this time?

Learn to discern the signs of the times.

57 Yea, and why even of yourselves judge ye not what is right?

58 When thou goest with thine adversary to the magistrate, *as thou art* in the way, give diligence that thou mayest be delivered from him; lest he hale thee to the judge, and the judge deliver thee to the officer, and the officer cast thee into prison.

Make peace, if possible, with your adversary.

59 I tell thee, thou shalt not depart thence, till thou hast paid the very last mite.

LUKE 13: 1-9

THERE were present at that season some that told him of the Galileans, whose blood Pilate had mingled with their sacrifices.

Repent of evil, or perish.

2 And Jesus, answering, said unto them, Suppose ye that these Galileans were sinners above all the Galileans, because they suffered such things?

*Suffering and accidents do **not** prove some people are more evil than others.*

3 I tell you, Nay; but, except ye repent, ye shall all likewise perish.

Or those eighteen upon whom the tower in Siloam fell, and slew them, think ye that they were sinners above all men that dwelt in Jerusalem?

5 I tell you, Nay; but except ye repent, ye shall all likewise perish.

6 He spake also this parable: A certain *man* had a fig-tree planted in his vineyard; and he came and sought fruit thereon, and found none.

Parable of the Barren Fig Tree.

7 Then said he unto the dresser of his vineyard, Behold, these three years I come seeking fruit on this fig-tree, and find none: cut it down; why cumbereth it the ground?

8 And he, answering, said unto him, Lord, let it alone this year also, till I shall dig about it, and dung *it:*

9 And if it bear fruit, *well:* and if not, *then* after that thou shalt cut it down.

LUKE 11: 37-41

37 And as he spake, a certain Pharisee besought him to dine with him: and he went in, and sat down to meat.

Precepts:

38 And when the Pharisee saw *it,* he marvelled that he had not first washed before dinner.

39 And the Lord said unto him, Now do ye Pharisees make clean the outside of the cup and the platter; but your inward part is full of ravening and wickedness.

Spiritual (internal) cleanliness is more important than external cleanliness.

40 *Ye* fools! did not he that made that which is without, make that which is within also?

41 But rather give alms of such things as ye have; and, behold, all things are clean unto you.

LUKE 11: 42-46, 52-54

42 But woe unto you, Pharisees! for ye tithe the mint, and rue, and all manner of herbs, and pass over judgment and the love of God: these ought ye to have done, and not to leave the other undone.

Be diligent not to forget judgment (justice) and love for God.

43 Woe unto you, Pharisees! for ye love the uppermost seats in the synagogues, and greetings in the markets.

44 Woe unto you, scribes and Pharisees, hypocrites! for ye are as graves which appear not, and the men that walk over *them* are not aware *of them.*

45 Then answered one of the lawyers, and said unto him, Master, thus saying, thou reproachest us also.

46 And he said, Woe unto you also, *ye* lawyers! for ye lade men with burdens grievous to be borne, and ye yourselves touch not the burdens with one of your fingers.

Don't hinder the learning of others.

52 Woe unto you, lawyers! for ye have taken away the key of knowledge: ye entered not in yourselves, and them that were entering in ye hindered.

53 And he said these things unto them, the scribes and the Pharisees began to urge *him* vehemently, and to provoke him to speak of many things;

54 Laying wait for him, and seeking to catch something out of his mouth, that they might accuse him.

MATT. 13: 1-4

THE same day went Jesus out of the house, and sat by the sea side.

Parable of the Sower.

2 And great multitudes were gathered together unto him, so that he went into a ship and sat; and the whole multitude stood on the shore.

3 And he spake many things unto them in parables, saying, Behold, a sower went forth to sow;

4 And, when he sowed, some *seeds* fell by the way-side, and the fowls came and devoured them.

MATT. 13: 5-9

5 Some fell upon stony places, where they had not much earth: and forthwith they sprung up, because they had no deepness of earth:
6 And when the sun was up, they were scorched: and, because they had not root, they withered away.
7 And some fell among thorns; and the thorns sprung up and choked them:
8 But other fell into good ground, and brought forth fruit, some an hundred-fold, some sixty-fold, some thirty-fold.
9 Who hath ears to hear, let him hear.

MARK 4: 10

10 And when he was alone, they that were ut him, with the twelve, asked of him parable.

MATT. 13: 18-23

Parable explained.

18 Hear ye, therefore, the parable of the sower.
19 When any one heareth the word of the kingdom, and understandeth *it* not, *then* cometh the wicked *one,* and catcheth away that which was sown in his heart. This is he which received seed by the way *side.*
20 But he that received the seed into stony places, the same is he that heareth the word, and anon with joy receiveth it;
21 Yet hath he not root in himself, but dureth for a while; for when tribulation or persecution ariseth because of the word, by and by he is offended.
22 He also that received seed among the thorns, is he that heareth the word; and the care of this world, and the deceitful-ness of riches, choke the word, and he becometh unfruitful.
23 But he that received seed into the good ground, is he that heareth the word and understandeth *it;* which also beareth fruit, and bringeth forth, some an hundred-fold, some sixty, some thirty.

MARK 4: 21-23

21 And he said unto them, Is a candle brought to be put under a bushel, or under a bed, and not to be set on a candlestick?
22 For there is nothing hid which shall not be manifested; neither was any thing kept secret, but that it should come abroad.
23 If any man have ears to hear, let him hear.

Parable of the Lamp Under a Basket.

MATT. 13: 24-30

24 Another parable put he forth unto them, saying, The kingdom of heaven is likened unto a man which sowed good seed in his field:
25 But, while men slept, his enemy came and sowed tares among the wheat, and went his way.
26 But when the blade was sprung up, and brought forth fruit, then appeared the tares also.
27 So the servants of the householder came and said unto him, Sir, didst not thou sow good seed in thy field? from whence then hath it tares?
28 He said unto them, An enemy hath done this. The servents said unto him, Wilt thou then that we go and gather them up?
29 But he said, Nay; lest, while ye gather up the tares, ye root up also the wheat with them.
30 Let both grow together until the harvest; and in the time of harvest I will say to the reapers, Gather ye together first the tares, and bind them in bundles to burn them: but gather the wheat into my barn.

Parable of the Wheat and the Tares.

MATT. 13: 36-38

36 Then Jesus sent the multitude away, and went into the house: and his disciples came unto him, saying, Declare unto us the parable of the tares of the field.
37 He answered and said unto them, He that soweth the good seed is the Son of Man;
38 The field is the world; the good seed are the children of the kingdom; but the tares are the children of the wicked *one;*

Parable explained.

MATT. 13: 39-52

39 The enemy that sowed them is the devil; the harvest is the end of the world: and the reapers are the angels.
40 As, therefore, the tares are gathered and burned in the fire; so shall it be in the end of this world.
41 The Son of Man shall send forth his angels, and they shall gather out of his kingdom all things that offend, and them which do iniquity;
42 And shall cast them into a furnace of fire: there shall be wailing and gnashing of teeth.
43 Then shall the righteous shine forth as the sun in the kingdom of their Father. Who hath ears to hear, let him hear.

Parable of the Hidden Treasure.

44 Again, the kingdom of heaven is like unto treasure hid in a field; the which when a man hath found he hideth, and, for joy thereof, goeth and selleth all that he hath, and buyeth that field.

Parable of the Pearl of Great Price.

45 Again, the kingdom of heaven is like unto a merchantman, seeking goodly pearls:
46 Who, when he had found one pearl of great price, went and sold all that he had, and bought it.

Parable of the Dragnet.

47 Again, the kingdom of heaven is like unto a net, that was cast into the sea, and gathered of every kind:
48 Which, when it was full, they drew to shore, and sat down, and gathered the good into vessels, but cast the bad away.
49 So shall it be at the end of the world: the angels shall come forth, and sever the wicked from among the just.
50 And, shall cast them into the furnace of fire: there shall be wailing and gnashing of teeth.
51 **Jesus saith unto them,** Have ye understood all these things? **They say unto him, Yea, Lord.**

Parable of the Householder.

52 **Then said he unto them,** Therefore every scribe *which is* instructed unto the kingdom of heaven is like unto a man *that is* an householder, which bringeth forth out of his treasure *things* new and old.

MARK 4: 26-34

26 And he said, So is the kingdom of God, as if a man should cast seed into the ground;
27 And should sleep, and rise night and day, and the seed should spring and grow up, he knoweth not how.
28 For the earth bringeth forth fruit of herself; first the blade, then the ear, after that the full corn in the ear.
29 But when the fruit is brought forth, immediately he putteth in the sickle, because the harvest is come.

Parable of the Growing Seed.

30 And he said, Whereunto shall we liken the kingdom of God? or with what comparison shall we compare it?
31 *It is* like a grain of mustard seed, which, when it is sown in the earth, is less than all the seeds that be in the earth:
32 But when it is sown, it groweth up, and becometh greater than all herbs, and shooteth out great branches; so that the fowls of the air may lodge under the shadow of it.
33 And with many such parables spake he the word unto them, as they were able to hear *it.*
34 But without a parable spake he not unto them: and when they were alone, he expounded all things to his disciples.

Parable of the Mustard Seed.

LUKE 9: 57-62

57 And it came to pass, that, as they went in the way, a certain *man* said unto him, Lord, I will follow thee whithersoever thou goest.
58 And Jesus said unto him, Foxes have holes, and birds of the air *have* nests; but the Son of Man hath not where to lay *his* head.
59 And he said unto another, Follow me. But he said, Lord, suffer me first to go and bury my father.

Let the dead bury their dead: but go thou and preach the kingdom of God.
61 And another also said, Lord, I will follow thee: but let me first go bid them farewell, which are at home at my house.
62 And Jesus said unto him, No man having put his hand to the plough, and looking back, is fit for the kingdom of God.

Costs of discipleship.

Count the cost before your decision to follow Christ.

LUKE 5: 27-29

27 And after these things, he went forth, and saw a publican, named Levi, sitting at the receipt of custom: and he said unto him, Follow me.

Sinners need to repent.

28 And he left all, rose up, and followed him.

29 And Levi made him a great feast in his own house:

MARK 2: 15-17

15 And many publicans and sinners sat also together with Jesus and his disciples: for there were many, and they followed him.

16 And when the scribes and Pharisees saw him eat with publicans and sinners, they said unto his disciples, How is it that he eateth and drinketh with publicans and sinners?

17 When Jesus heard *it*, he saith unto them, They that are whole have no need of the physician, but they that are sick: I came not to call the righteous, but sinners to repentance.

LUKE 5: 36-38

36 And he spake also a parable unto them; No man putteth a piece of a new garment upon an old; if otherwise, then both the new maketh a rent, and the piece that was *taken* out of the new agreeth not with the old.

Parable of New Cloth.

37 And no man putteth new wine into old bottles; else the new wine will burst the bottles, and be spilled, and the bottles shall perish.

Parable of New Wine in Old Bottles.

But new wine must be put into new bottles; and both are preserved.

MATT. 13: 53-56

53 And it came to pass, *that* when Jesus had finished these parables, he departed thence.

A prophet has no honor in his own country.

54 And when he was come into his own country, he taught them in their synagogue, insomuch that they were astonished, and said, Whence hath this *man* this wisdom, and *these* mighty works?

55 Is not this the carpenter's son? is not his mother called Mary? and his brethren, James, and Joses, and Simon, and Judas?

56 And his sisters, are they not all with us? Whence then hath

this *man* all these things?

MATT. 13: 57

57 And they were offended in him. But Jesus said unto them, A prophet is not without honour, save in his own country, and in his own house.

MATT. 9: 36

36 But when he saw the multitudes, he was moved with compassion on them, because they fainted, and were scattered abroad, as sheep having no shepherd.

MARK 6: 7

7 And he calleth *unto him* the twelve, and began to send them forth by two and two;

MATT. 10: 5, 6, 9-17

Mission and instruction of the twelve apostles.

5 and commanded them, saying, Go not into the way of the Gentiles, and into *any* city of the Samaritans enter ye not:

6 But go rather to the lost sheep of the house of Israel.

9 Provide neither gold, nor silver, nor brass in your purses;

10 Nor scrip for your journey, neither two coats, neither shoes, nor yet staves: for the workman is worthy of his meat.

11 And into whatsoever city or town ye shall enter, enquire who in it is worthy; and there abide till ye go thence.

12 And when ye come into an house, salute it.

13 And if the house be worthy, let your peace come upon it: but if it be not worthy, let your peace return to you.

14 And whosoever shall not receive you, nor hear your words, when ye depart out of that house, or city, shake off the dust of your feet.

15 Verily I say unto you, It shall be more tolerable for the land of Sodom and Gomorrha, in the day of judgment, than for that city.

16 Behold, I send you forth as sheep in the midst of wolves: be ye, therefore, wise as serpents, and harmless as doves.

17 But beware of men: for they will deliver you up to the councils, and they will scourge you

in their synagogues:

MATT. 10: 18, 23, 26-31

18 And ye shall be brought before governors and kings for my sake, for a testimony against them and the Gentiles.
23 But when they persecute you in this city, flee ye into another:
26 Fear them not, therefore: for there is nothing covered that shall not be revealed; and hid, that shall not be known.
27 What I tell you in darkness, *that* speak ye in light: and what ye hear in the ear, *that* preach ye upon the housetops.
28 And fear not them which kill the body, but are not able to kill the soul: but rather fear him which is able to destroy both soul and body in hell.
29 Are not two sparrows sold for a farthing? and one of them shall not fall on the ground without your Father.
30 But the very hairs of your head are all numbered.
31 Fear ye not, therefore, ye are of more value than many sparrows.

MARK 6: 12, 30

12 And they went out, and preached that men should repent.

The apostles report back to Jesus.

30 And the apostles gathered themselves together unto Jesus, and told him all things, both what they had done, and what they had taught.

JOHN 7: 1

Precepts:

AFTER these things Jesus walked in Galilee: for he would not walk in Jewry, because the Jews sought to kill him.

MARK 7: 1-3

THEN came together unto him, the Pharisees, and certain of the scribes, which came from Jerusalem.
2 And when they saw some of his disciples eat bread with defiled (that is to say, with unwashen) hands, they found fault.
3 For the Pharisees, and all the Jews, except they wash *their* hands oft, eat not, holding the tradition of the elders.

MARK 7: 4, 5

4 And *when they come* from the market, except they wash, they eat not. And many other things there be, which they have received to hold, *as* the washing of cups, and pots, and of brasen vessels, and tables.
5 Then the Pharisees and scribes asked him, Why walk not thy disciples according to the tradition of the elders, but eat bread with unwashen hands?

MARK 7: 14-24

14 And, when he had called all the people *unto him,* he said unto them, Hearken unto me every one *of you,* and understand:
15 There is nothing from without a man, that entering into him can defile him: but the things which come out of him, those are they that defile the man.

Man is defiled by evil thoughts, not by food.

16 If any man have ears to hear, let him hear.
17 And, when he was entered into the house from the people, his disciples asked him concerning the parable.
18 And he saith unto them, Are ye so without understanding also? Do ye not perceive, that whatsoever thing from without entereth into the man, *it* cannot defile him;
19 Because it entereth not into his heart, but into the belly, and goeth out into the draught, purging all meats?
20 And he said, That which cometh out of the man, that defileth the man.
21 For from within, out of the heart of men, proceed evil thoughts, adulteries, fornications, murders,
22 Thefts, covetousness, wickedness, deceit, lasciviousness, an evil eye, blasphemy, pride, foolishness:
23 All these evil things come from within, and defile the man.
24 And from thence he arose, and went into the borders of Tyre and Sidon, and entered into an house, and would have no man know *it:* but he could not be hid.

MATT. 18: 1-4	AT the same time came the disciples unto Jesus, saying, Who is the greatest in the kingdom of heaven? 2 And Jesus called a little child unto him, and set him in the midst of them, 3 And said, Verily I say unto you, Except ye be converted, and become as little children, ye shall not enter into the kingdom of heaven. 4 Whosoever, therefore, shall humble himself as this little child, the same is greatest in the kingdom of heaven.	*Become like a little child – humble.*
MATT. 18: 7-9	7 Woe unto the world because of offences! for it must needs be that offences come; but woe to that man by whom the offence cometh!	*Don't be an offensive person.*
	8 Wherefore, if thy hand or thy foot offend thee, cut them off, and cast *them* from thee: it is better for thee to enter into life halt or maimed, rather than having two hands, or two feet, to be cast into everlasting fire. 9 And if thine eye offend thee, pluck it out, and cast *it* from thee: it is better for thee to enter into life with one eye, rather than having two eyes to be cast into hell-fire.	*Avoid those situations that cause one to sin.*
MATT. 18: 12-15	12 How think ye? if a man have an hundred sheep, and one of them be gone astray, doth he not leave the ninety and nine, and goeth into the mountains, and seeketh that which is gone astray? 13 And if so be that he find it, verily I say unto you, He rejoiceth more of that *sheep*, than of the ninety and nine which went not astray. 14 Even so it is not the will of your Father which is in heaven, that one of these little ones should perish.	*God doesn't want to "lose" anyone.*
	15 Moreover, if thy brother shall trespass against thee, go and tell him his fault between thee and him alone; if he shall hear thee,	*Resolve to solve offenses:* *1. Person to person.*

thou hast gained thy brother.

MATT. 18: 16, 17

16 But if he will not hear *thee, then* take with thee one or two more, that in the mouth of two or three witnesses every word may be established.

2. Use Witnesses.

17 And if he shall neglect to hear them, tell *it* unto the church: but if he neglect to hear the church, let him be unto thee as an heathen man and a publican.

3. Use The Church.

MATT. 18: 21, 22

21 Then came Peter to him, and said, Lord, how oft shall my brother sin against me, and I forgive him? till seven times?

Forgiveness has no limits.

22 Jesus saith unto him, I say not unto thee, Until seven times; but, Until seventy times seven.

MATT. 18: 23-30

23 Therefore is the kingdom of heaven likened unto a certain king, which would take account of his servents.

Parable of the Unforgiving Servant.

24 And when he had begun to reckon, one was brought unto him, which owed him ten thousand talents.

25 But forasmuch as he had not to pay, his lord commanded him to be sold, and his wife, and children, and all that he had, and payment to be made.

26 The servant, therefore fell down, and worshipped him, saying, lord, have patience with me, and I will pay thee all.

27 Then the lord of that servant was moved with compassion, and loosed him, and forgave him the debt.

28 But the same servant went out, and found one of his fellow-servants, which owed him an hundred pence: and he laid hands on him, and took *him* by the throat, saying, Pay me that thou owest.

29 And his fellow-servant fell down at his feet, and besought him, saying, Have patience with me, and I will pay thee all.

30 And he would not: but went and cast him into prison, till he should pay the debt.

MATT. 18: 31-35

31 So when his fellow-servants saw what was done, they were very sorry, and came and told unto their lord all that was done.
32 Then his lord, after that he had called him, said unto him, O thou wicked servant! I forgave thee all that debt, because thou desiredst me:
33 Shouldest not thou also have had compassion on thy fellow-servant, even as I had pity on thee?

Forgiveness is an essential trait of God's people.

34 And his lord was wroth, and delivered him to the tormentors, till he should pay all that was due unto him.
35 So likewise shall my heavenly Father do also unto you, if ye from your hearts forgive not every one his brother their trespasses.

LUKE 10: 1-8

Mission of the seventy disciples.

AFTER these things the Lord appointed other seventy also, and sent them two and two before his face into every city and place, whither he himself would come.
2 Therefore said he unto them, The harvest truly *is* great, but the labourers *are* few: pray ye therefore the lord of the harvest, that he would send forth labourers into his harvest.
3 Go your ways: behold, I send you forth as lambs among wolves.
4 Carry neither purse, nor scrip, nor shoes: and salute no man by the way.
5 And into whatsoever house ye enter, first say, Peace *be* to this house.
6 And if the Son of Peace be there, your peace shall rest upon it: if not, it shall turn to you again.
7 And in the same house remain, eating and drinking such things as they give: for the labourer is worthy of his hire. Go not from house to house.
8 And into whatsoever city ye enter, and they receive you, eat such things as are set before you;

LUKE 10: 10-12

10 But into whatsoever city ye enter, and they receive you not, go your ways out into the streets of the same, and say,
11 Even the very dust of your city, which cleaveth on us, we do wipe off against you: notwithstanding, be ye sure of this, that the kingdom of God is come nigh unto you.
12 But I say unto you, That is shall be more tolerable in that day for Sodom, than for that city.

JOHN 7: 2-16

Jesus attends the fall festival – the Feast of Tabernacles.

2 Now the Jews' feast of tabernacles was at hand.
3 His brethren, therefore, said unto him, Depart hence, and go into Judea, that thy disciples also may see the works that thou doest.
4 For *there is* no man *that* doeth any thing in secret, and he himself seeketh to be known openly. If thou do these things, shew thyself to the world.
5 For neither did his brethren believe in him.
6 Then Jesus said unto them, My time is not yet come: but your time is alway ready.
7 The world cannot hate you: but me it hateth, because I testify of it, that the works thereof are evil.
8 Go ye up unto this feast: I go not up yet unto this feast; for my time is not yet full come.
9 When he had said these words unto them, he abode *still* in Galilee.
10 But when his brethren were gone up, then went he also up unto the feast, not openly, but as it were in secret.
11 Then the Jews sought him at the feast, and said, Where is he?
12 And there was much murmuring among the people concerning him: for some said, He is a good man: others said, Nay; but he deceiveth the people.
13 Howbeit no man spake openly of him for fear of the Jews.
14 Now, about the midst of the feast, Jesus went up into the temple, and taught.
15 And the Jews marvelled, saying, How knoweth this man letters having never learned?
16 Jesus answered them, and said,

JOHN 7: 19-26

19 Did not Moses give you the law, and *yet* none of you keepeth the law? Why go ye about to kill me?
20 The people answered, and said, Thou hast a devil: who goeth about to kill thee?
21 Jesus answered, and said unto them, I have done one work, and ye all marvel.
22 Moses, therefore, gave unto you circumcision, (not because it is of Moses, but of the fathers,) and ye on the sabbath-day circumcise a man.
23 If a man on the sabbath-day receive circumcision, that the law of Moses should not be broken; are ye angry at me, because I have made a man every whit whole on the sabbath-day?
24 Judge not according to the appearance, but judge righteous judgment.
25 Then said some of them of Jerusalem, Is not this he whom they seek to kill?
26 But, lo, he speaketh boldly, and they say nothing unto him; Do the rulers know indeed that this is the very Christ?

Jesus disputes with the Jews.

Jesus: Judge not according to appearances.

JOHN 7: 32

32 The Pharisees heard that the people murmured such things concerning him; and the Pharisees, and the chief priest sent officers to take him.

JOHN 7: 43-49

43 So there was a division among the people because of him.
44 And some of them would have taken him: but no man laid hands on him.
45 Then came the officers to the chief priests and Pharisees; and they said unto them, Why have ye not brought him?
46 The officers answered, Never man spake like this man.
47 Then answered them the Pharisees, Are ye also deceived?
48 Have any of the rulers, or of the Pharisees, believed on him?
49 But this people who knoweth not the law are cursed.

JOHN 7: 50-53

Nicodemus defends Jesus.

50 Nicodemus saith unto them, (he that came to Jesus by night, being one of them,)
51 Doth our law judge *any* man, before it hear him, and know what he doeth?
52 They answered, and said unto him, Art thou also of Galilee? Search and look: for out of Galilee ariseth no prophet.
53 And every man went unto his own house.

JOHN 8: 1-11

A woman taken in adultery.

JESUS went unto the mount of Olives.
2 And early in the morning he came again into the temple, and all the people came unto him: and he sat down, and taught them.
3 And the scribes and Pharisees brought unto him a woman taken in adultery; and, when they had set her in the midst,
4 They say unto him, Master, this woman was taken in adultery, in the very act.
5 Now Moses in the law commanded us, That such should be stoned: but what sayest thou?
6 This they said, tempting him, that they might have to accuse him. But Jesus stooped down, and with *his* finger wrote on the ground, *as though he heard them not.*
7 So, when they continued asking him, he lifted up himself, and said unto them, He that is without sin among you, let him first cast a stone at her.
8 And again he stooped down, and wrote on the ground.
9 And they which heard *it,* being convicted by *their own* conscience, went out one by one, beginning at the eldest, *even* unto the last; and Jesus was left alone, and the woman standing in the midst.

Jesus' response: Sin no more.

10 When Jesus had lifted up himself, and saw none but the woman, he said unto her, Woman, where are those thine accusers? hath no man condemned thee?
11 She said, No man, Lord. And Jesus said unto her, Neither do I condemn thee: go, and sin no more.

JOHN 9: 1-3	AND as *Jesus* passed by, he saw a man which was blind from *his* birth. 2 And his disciples asked him, saying, Master, who did sin, this man, or his parents, that he was born blind? 3 Jesus answered, Neither hath this man sinned, nor his parents: but that the works of God should be made manifest in him.	*To be born blind is no proof of sin.*
JOHN 10: 1-5	VERILY, verily, I say unto you, He that entereth not by the door into the sheepfold, but climbeth up some other way, the same is a thief and a robber. 2 But he that entereth in by the door, is the shepherd of the sheep. 3 To him the porter openeth; and the sheep hear his voice: and he calleth his own sheep by name, and leadeth them out. 4 And when he putteth forth his own sheep, he goeth before them, and the sheep follow him: for they know his voice. 5 And a stranger will they not follow, but will flee from him: for they know not the voice of strangers.	*Difference between a shepherd and a thief.*
JOHN 10: 11-14, 16	11 I am the good shepherd: the good shepherd giveth his life for the sheep. 12 But he that is an hireling, and not the shepherd, whose own the sheep are not, seeth the wolf coming, and leaveth the sheep, and fleeth: and the wolf catcheth them, and scattereth the sheep. 13 The hireling fleeth, because he is an hireling, and careth not for the sheep. 14 I am the good shepherd, and know my *sheep*, and am known of mine. 16 And other sheep I have, which are not of this fold: them also I must bring, and they shall hear my voice; and there shall be one fold, *and* one shepherd.	*Jesus identifies Himself as the Good Shepherd.*

LUKE 10:
25-37

Love God and your neighbor.

25 And, behold, a certain lawyer stood up, and tempted him, saying, Master, what shall I do to inherit eternal life?
26 He said unto him, What is written in the law? how readest thou?
27 And he answering, said, Thou shalt love the Lord thy God with all thy heart, and with all thy soul, and with all thy strength, and with all thy mind; and thy neighbour as thyself.
28 And he said unto him, Thou hast answered right: this do, and thou shalt live.
29 But he, willing to justify himself, said unto Jesus, And who is my neighbour?

Parable of the Good Samaritan.

30 And Jesus, answering, said, A certain *man* went down from Jerusalem to Jericho, and fell among thieves, which stripped him of his raiment, and wounded *him,* and departed, leaving *him* half dead.
31 And, by chance, there came down a certain priest that way; and when he saw him, he passed by on the other side.
32 And likewise a Levite, when he was at the place, came and looked *on him,* and passed by on the other side.
33 But a certain Samaritan, as he journeyed, came where he was: and when he saw him, he had compassion *on him.*
34 And went to *him,* and bound up his wounds, pouring in oil and wine, and set him on his own beast, and brought him to an inn, and took care of him.
35 And on the morrow, when he departed, he took out two pence, and gave *them* to the host, and said unto him, Take care of him: and whatsoever thou spendest more, when I come again, I will repay thee.
36 Which now of these three, thinkest thou was neighbour unto him that fell among the thieves?
37 And he said, He that shewed mercy on him. Then said Jesus unto him, Go, and do thou likewise.

LUKE 11: 1-12

AND it came to pass, that, as he was praying in a certain place, when he ceased, one of his disciples said unto him, Lord, teach us to pray, as John also taught his disciples.

A model or form for prayer – "The Lord's Prayer."

2 And he said unto them, When ye pray, say, Our Father, which art in heaven: Hallowed be thy name. Thy kingdom come. Thy will be done, as in heaven, so in earth.
3 Give us day by day our daily bread.
4 And forgive us our sins; for we also forgive every one that is indebted to us. And lead us not into temptation; but deliver us from evil.

5 And he said unto them, Which of you shall have a friend, and shall go unto him at midnight, and say unto him, Friend, lend me three loaves;

Parable of the Friend at Midnight.

6 For a friend of mine in his journey is come to me, and I have nothing to set before him?
7 And he from within shall answer, and say, Trouble me not: the door is now shut, and my children are with me in bed; I cannot rise and give thee.
8 I say unto you, Though he will not rise and give him, because he is his friend; yet because of his importunity he will rise and give him as many as he needeth.

9 And I say unto you, Ask, and it shall be given you; seek, and ye shall find: knock, and it shall be opened unto you.

Keep asking, seeking, and knocking for spiritual understanding.

10 For every one that asketh, receiveth; and he that seeketh, findeth; and to him that knocketh, it shall be opened.
11 If a son shall ask bread of any of you that is a father, will he give him a stone? or if *he ask* a fish, will he for a fish give him a serpent?
12 Or, if he shall ask an egg, will he offer him a scorpion?

LUKE 11: 13

13 If ye then, being evil, know how to give good gifts unto your children; how much more shall *your* heavenly Father give the Holy Spirit to them that ask him?

LUKE 14: 1-6

Jesus indicates appropriateness of healing on the Sabbath.

AND it came to pass, as he went into the house of one of the chief Pharisees to eat bread on the sabbath-day, that they watched him.

2 And, behold, there was a certain man before him, which had the dropsy.

3 And Jesus, answering, spake unto the lawyers and Pharisees, saying, Is it lawful to heal on the sabbath-day?

4 And they held their peace.

5 And he saith unto them, Which of you shall have an ass or an ox fallen into a pit, and will not straightway pull him out on the sabbath-day?

6 And they could not answer him again to these things.

LUKE 14: 7-12

Parable of Those Invited to a Wedding Feast.

7 And he put forth a parable to those which were bidden, when he marked how they chose out the chief rooms; saying unto them,

8 When thou art bidden of any *man* to a wedding, sit not down in the highest room; lest a more honourable man than thou be bidden of him;

9 And he that bade thee and him, come and say to thee, Give this man place; and thou begin with shame to take the lowest room.

10 But when thou art bidden, go and sit down in the lowest room; that when he that bade thee cometh, he may say unto thee, Friend, go up higher: then shalt thou have worship in the presence of them that sit at meat with thee.

Principle: He who exalts himself shall be abased; he who humbles himself shall be exalted.

11 For whosoever exalteth himself shall be abased; and he that humbleth himself shall be exalted.

12 Then said he also to him that bade him, When thou makest a dinner or a supper, call not thy friends, nor thy brethren, neither thy kinsmen, nor thy rich neighbours; lest they also bid thee again, and a recompense be made thee.

LUKE 14: 13-14, 16-24

13 But when thou makest a feast, call the poor, the maimed, the lame, the blind:
14 And thou shalt be blessed; for they cannot recompense thee: for thou shalt be recompensed at the resurrection of the just.

Parable of the Great Supper.

16 Then said he unto him, A certain man made a great supper, and bade many:
17 And sent his servant at supper-time to say to them that were bidden, Come, for all things are now ready.
18 And they all with one *consent* began to make excuse. The first said unto him, I have bought a piece of ground, and I must needs go and see it: I pray thee have me excused.
19 And another said, I have bought five yoke of oxen, and I go to prove them: I pray thee have me excused.
20 And another said, I have married a wife; and therefore I cannot come.
21 So that servant came, and shewed his lord these things. Then the master of the house, being angry, said to his servant, Go out quickly into the streets and lanes of the city, and bring in hither the poor, and the maimed, and the halt, and the blind.
22 And the servant said, Lord, it is done as thou hast commanded, and yet there is room.
23 And the lord said unto the servant, Go out into the highways and hedges, and compel *them* to come in, that my house may be filled.
24 For I say unto you, That none of those men which were bidden, shall taste of my supper.

LUKE 14: 28-29

Precepts: Count the cost before any decision.

28 For which of you, intending to build a tower, sitteth not down first, and counteth the cost, whether he have *sufficient* to finish *it?*
29 Lest haply, after he hath laid the foundation, and is not able to finish *it* all that behold *it* begin to mock him,

LUKE 14: 30-32

30 Saying, This man began to build, and was not able to finish.
31 Or what king, going to make war against another king, sitteth not down first, and consulteth whether he be able with ten thousand to meet him that cometh against him with twenty thousand?
32 Or else, while the other is yet a great way off, he sendeth an ambassage, and desireth conditions of peace.

LUKE 15: 1-10

Parable of the Lost Sheep.

THEN drew near unto him all the publicans and sinners for to hear him.
2 And the Pharisees and scribes murmured, saying, This man receiveth sinners, and eateth with them.
3 And he spake this parable unto them, saying,
4 What man of you, having an hundred sheep, if he lose one of them, doth not leave the ninety and nine in the wilderness, and go after that which is lost, until he find it?
5 And when he hath found *it*, he layeth *it* on his shoulders, rejoicing.
6 And when he cometh home, he calleth together *his* friends and neighbours, saying unto them, Rejoice with me; for I have found my sheep which was lost.

Joy in Heaven over one repentent sinner.

7 I say unto you, That likewise joy shall be in heaven over one sinner that repenteth, more than over ninety and nine just persons, which need no repentance.

Parable of the Lost Coin.

8 Either what woman, having ten pieces of silver, if she lose one piece, doth not light a candle, and sweep the house, and seek diligently till she find *it?*
9 And when she hath found *it*, she calleth *her* friends and *her* neighbours together, saying, Rejoice with me; for I have found the piece which I had lost.
10 Likewise, I say unto you, There is joy in the presence of the angels of God, over one sinner that repenteth.

LUKE 15: 11-23

Parable of the Prodigal Son and His Brother.

11 And he said, A certain man had two sons:
12 And the younger of them said to *his* father, Father, give me the portion of goods that falleth *to me*. And he divided unto them *his* living.
13 And not many days after the younger son gathered all together, and took his journey into a far country, and there wasted his substance with riotous living.
14 And when he had spent all, there arose a mighty famine in that land; and he began to be in want.
15 And he went and joined himself to a citizen of that country; and he sent him into his fields to feed swine.
16 And he would fain to have filled his belly with the husks that the swine did eat: and no man gave unto him.
17 And when he came to himself, he said, How many hired servants of my father's have bread enough, and to spare, and I perish with hunger!
18 I will arise, and go to my father, and will say unto him, Father, I have sinned against heaven, and before thee,
19 And am no more worthy to be called thy son: make me as one of thy hired servants.
20 And he arose, and came to his father. But, when he was yet a great way off, his father saw him, and had compassion, and ran, and fell on his neck, and kissed him.
21 And the son said unto him, Father, I have sinned against heaven, and in thy sight, and am no more worthy to be called thy son.
22 But the father said to his servants, Bring forth the best robe, and put *it* on him; and put a ring on his hand, and shoes on *his* feet:
23 And bring hither the fatted calf, and kill *it;* and let us eat, and be merry:

LUKE 15: 24-32

Parable of the Prodigal Son and His Brother (continued)

24 For this my son was dead, and is alive again; he was lost, and is found. And they began to be merry.

25 Now, his elder son was in the field: and as he came and drew nigh to the house, he heard musick and dancing.

26 And he called one of the servants, and asked what these things meant.

27 And he said unto him, Thy brother is come; and thy father hath killed the fatted calf, because he hath received him safe and sound.

28 And he was angry, and would not go in: therefore came his father out, and entreated him.

29 And he, answering, said to *his* father, Lo, these many years do I serve thee, neither transgressed I at any time thy commandment; and yet thou never gavest me a kid, that I might make merry with my friends:

30 But as soon as this thy son was come, which hath devoured thy living with harlots, thou hast killed for him the fatted calf.

31 And he said unto him, Son, thou art ever with me, and all that I have is thine.

32 It was meet that we should make merry, and be glad: for this thy brother was dead, and is alive again; and was lost, and is found.

LUKE 16: 1-3

Parable of the Unjust Steward.

AND he said also unto his disciples, There was a certain rich man, which had a steward; and the same was accused unto him that he had wasted his goods.

2 And he called him, and said unto him, How is it that I hear this of thee? give an account of thy stewardship; for thou mayest be no longer steward.

3 Then the steward said within himself, What shall I do, for my lord taketh away from me the stewardship? I cannot dig; to beg I am ashamed.

LUKE 16:
4-15

4 I am resolved what to do, that when I am put out of the stewardship, they may receive me into their houses.
5 So he called every one of his lord's debtors *unto him*, and said unto the first, How much owest thou unto my lord?
6 And he said, An hundred measures of oil. And he said unto him, Take thy bill, and sit down quickly, and write fifty.
7 Then said he to another, And how much owest thou? And he said, An hundred measures of wheat. And he said unto him, Take thy bill, and write fourscore.
8 And the lord commended the unjust steward, because he had done wisely: for the children of this world are in their generation wiser than the children of light.
9 And I say unto you, Make to yourselves friends of the mammon of unrighteousness; that, when ye fail, they may receive you into everlasting habitations.
10 He that is faithful in that which is least, is faithful also in much; and he that is unjust in the least, is unjust also in much.

Person faithful in little, will be faithful in much.

11 If, therefore, ye have not been faithful in the unrighteous mammon, who will commit to your trust the true *riches?*
12 And if ye have not been faithful in that which is another man's, who shall give you that which is your own?
13 No servant can serve two masters: for either he will hate the one, and love the other; or else he will hold to the one, and despise the other. Ye cannot serve God and mammon.

One cannot serve God and money.

14 And the Pharisees also, who were covetous, heard all these things: and they derided him.
15 And he said unto them, Ye are they which justify yourselves before men; but God knoweth your hearts: for that which is highly esteemed among men is abomination in the sight of God.

LUKE 16: 18-29

18 Whosoever putteth away his wife, and marrieth another, committeth adultery: and whosoever marrieth her that is put away from *her* husband, committeth adultery.

Parable of Lazarus and the Rich Man.

19 There was a certain rich man, which was clothed in purple and fine linen, and fared sumptuously every day:

20 And there was a certain beggar, named Lazarus, which was laid at his gate full of sores,

21 And desiring to be fed with the crumbs which fell from the rich man's table: moreover, the dogs came and licked his sores.

22 And it came to pass, that the beggar died, and was carried by the angels into Abraham's bosom: the rich man also died, and was buried;

23 And in hell he lifted up his eyes, being in torments, and seeth Abraham afar off, and Lazarus in his bosom.

24 And he cried, and said, Father Abraham, have mercy on me; and send Lazarus, that he may dip the tip of his finger in water, and cool my tongue; for I am tormented in this flame.

25 But Abraham said, Son, remember that thou in thy life time receivedst thy good things, and likewise Lazarus evil things: but now he is comforted, and thou art tormented.

26 And, besides all this, between us and you there is a great gulf fixed: so that they which would pass from hence to you cannot; neither can they pass to us, that *would come* from thence.

27 And he said, I pray thee, therefore, father, that thou wouldest send him to my father's house:

28 For I have five brethren; that he may testify unto them, lest they also come into this place of torment.

29 Abraham saith unto him, They have Moses and the prophets; let them hear them.

LUKE 16: 30, 31

30 And he said, Nay, father Abraham: but if one went unto them from the dead, they will repent.

31 And he said unto him, If they hear not Moses and the prophets, neither will they be persuaded though one rose from the dead.

LUKE 17: 1-4

THEN said he unto the disciples, It is impossible but that offences will come: but woe *unto him* through whom they come?

If a person repents, forgive him.

2 It were better for him that a mill-stone were hanged about his neck, and he cast into the sea, than that he should offend one of these little ones.

3 Take heed to yourselves: If thy brother trespass against thee, rebuke him; and if he repent, forgive him.

4 And if he trespass against thee seven times in a day, and seven times in a day turn again to thee, saying, I repent; thou shalt forgive him.

LUKE 17: 7-10

7 But which of you having a servant plowing, or feeding cattle, will say unto him by and by, when he is come from the field, Go and sit down to meat?

Parable of the Unprofitable Servant.

8 And will not rather say unto him, Make ready wherewith I may sup, and gird thyself, and serve me, till I have eaten and drunken; and afterward thou shalt eat and drink?

9 Doth he thank that servant because he did the things that were commanded him? I trow not.

Profitable persons go beyond their duty.

10 So likewise ye, when ye shall have done all those things which are commanded you, say, We are unprofitable servants: we have done that which was our duty to do.

LUKE 17: 20

20 And when he was demanded of the Pharisees, when the kingdom of God should come, he answered them, and said, The kingdom of God cometh not with observation.

Always be ready.

LUKE 17: 26-36	**26** And as it was in the days of Noe, so shall it be also in the days of the Son of Man: **27** They did eat, they drank, they married wives, they were given in marriage, until the day that Noe entered into the ark; and the flood came, and destroyed them all. **28** Likewise also, as it was in the days of Lot, they did eat, they drank, they bought, they sold, they planted, they builded: **29** But the same day that Lot went out of Sodom, it rained fire and brimstone from heaven, and destroyed *them* all. **30** Even thus shall it be in the day when the Son of Man is revealed. **31** In that day, he which shall be upon the house-top, and his stuff in the house, let him not come down to take it away: and he that is in the field, let him likewise not return back. **32** Remember Lot's wife. **33** Whosoever shall seek to save his life shall lose it; and whosoever shall lose his life shall preserve it. **34** I tell you, in that night there shall be two *men* in one bed; the one shall be taken, and the other shall be left. **35** Two *women* will be grinding together; the one shall be taken, and the other left. **36** Two *men* shall be in the field; the one shall be taken, and the other left.	*The scenario for Christ's return.*
LUKE 18: 1-3	**AND he spake a parable unto them, *to this end*, that men ought always *to* pray, and not to faint;** **2 Saying,** There was in a city a judge, which feared not God, neither regarded man: **3** And there was a widow in that city; and she came unto him, saying, Avenge me of mine adversary.	*Pray always, don't lose heart.* *Parable of the Persistent Widow and Unjust Judge.*

LUKE 18: 4-14

4 And he would not for a while: but afterward he said within himself, Though I fear not God, nor regard man;
5 Yet, because this widow troubleth me, I will avenge her, lest by her continual coming she weary me.
6 And the Lord said, Hear what the unjust judge saith.
7 And shall not God avenge his own elect, which cry day and night unto him, though he bear long with them?

God will avenge His own.

8 I tell you, that he will avenge them speedily. Nevertheless, when the Son of Man cometh, shall he find faith on the earth?
9 And he spake this parable unto certain which trusted in themselves, that they were righteous, and despised others:

Parable of the Pharisee and Tax Collector.

10 Two men went up into the temple to pray; the one a Pharisee, and the other a publican.
11 The Pharisee stood and prayed thus with himself, God, I thank thee, that I am not as other men*are,* extortioners, unjust, adulterers, or even as this publican.
12 I fast twice in the week, I give tithes of all that I possess.
13 And the publican, standing afar off, would not lift up so much as*his* eyes unto heaven, but smote upon his breast, saying, God be merciful to me a sinner.
14 I tell you, this man went down to his house justified *rather* than the other: for every one that exalteth himself shall be abased; and he that humbleth himself shall be exalted.

Those who exalt themselves shall be abased; the humble shall be exalted.

LUKE 10: 38-40

38 Now it came to pass, as they went, that he entered into a certain village: and a certain woman, named Martha, received him into her house.
39 And she had a sister called Mary, which also sat at Jesus' feet, and heard his word.
40 But .Martha was cumbered

LUKE 10: 40-42

about much serving, and came to him, and said, Lord, dost thou not care that my sister hath left me to serve alone? bid her, therefore, that she help me.

41 And Jesus answered, and said unto her, Martha, Martha, thou art careful, and troubled about many things:

42 But one thing is needful: and Mary hath chosen that good part, which shall not be taken away from her.

Learn to prioritize.

MATT. 19: 1-10

AND it came to pass *that,* when Jesus had finished these sayings, he departed from Galilee, and came into the coasts of Judea beyond Jordan:

2 And great multitudes followed him,

3 The Pharisees also came unto him, tempting him, and saying unto him, Is it lawful for a man to put away his wife for every cause?

4 And he answered and said unto them, Have ye not read, that he which made *them* at the beginning, made them male and female?

5 And said, For this cause shall a man leave father and mother, and shall cleave to his wife; and they twain shall be one flesh.

6 Wherefore they are no more twain, but one flesh. What, therefore, God hath joined together, let no man put asunder.

God did not purpose divorce.

7 They say unto him, Why did Moses then command to give a writing of divorcement, and to put her away?

8 He saith unto them, Moses, because of the hardness of your hearts, suffered you to put away your wives: but from the beginning it was not so.

9 And I say unto you, Whosoever shall put away his wife, except *it be* for fornication, and shall marry another, committeth adultery: and whoso marrieth her which is put away doth commit adultery.

Divorce, except for fornication, and remarriage constitutes adultery.

10 His disciples say unto him, If the case of the man be so with *his* wife, it is not good to marry.

MATT. 19: 11-25

11 But he said unto them, All *men* cannot receive this saying, save*they* to whom it is given.

12 For there are some eunuchs, which were so born from *their* of heaven's sake. He that is able to receive*it,* let him receive *it.*

13 Then were there brought unto him little children, that he should put *his* hands on them and pray: and the disciples rebuked them.

14 Suffer little children, and forbid them not, to come unto me: for of such is the kingdom of heaven.

Those in the Kingdom will be childlike.

15 And he laid *his* hands on them, and departed thence.

16 And, behold, one came and said unto him, Good Master, what good thing shall I do, that I may have eternal life?

17 And he said uto him, Why callest thou me good? *there is* none good but one, *that is,* God: but if thou wilt enter into life, keep the commandments.

Christians keep the Ten Commandments.

18 He saith unto him, Which? Jesus said, Thou shalt do no murder, Thou shalt not commit adultery, Thou shalt not steal, Thou shalt not bear false witness,

19 Honour thy father and *thy* mother: and, Thou shalt love thy neighbour as thyself.

20 The young man saith unto him, All these things I have kept from my youth up: what lack I yet?

21 Jesus said unto him, If thou wilt be perfect, go*and* sell that thou hast, and give to the poor, and thou shalt have treasure in heaven; and come *and* follow me.

22 But when the young man heard that saying, he went away sorrowful: for he had great possessions.

23 Then said Jesus unto his disciples, Verily I say unto you, That a rich man shall hardly enter into the kingdom of heaven.

24 And again I say unto you, It is easier for a camel to go through the eye of a needle, than for a rich man to enter into the kingdom of God.

Rich people find it difficult to keep God first.

25 When his disciples heard *it,*

MATT. 19: 26

they were exceedingly amazed, saying, Who then can be saved?

26 But Jesus beheld *them,* and said unto them, With men this is impossible; but with God all things are possible.

MATT. 20: 1-12

Parable of the Laborers in the Vineyard.

FOR the kingdom of heaven is like unto a man *that is* an householder, which went out early in the morning to hire labourers into his vineyard.

2 And when he had agreed with the labourers for a penny a day, he sent them into his vineyard.

3 And he went out about the third hour, and saw others standing idle in the market-place,

4 And said unto them, Go ye also into the vineyard; and whatsoever is right I will give you. And they went their way.

5 Again he went out about the sixth and ninth hour, and did likewise.

6 And about the eleventh hour he went out, and found others standing idle, and saith unto them, Why stand ye here all the day idle?

7 They say unto him, Because no man hath hired us. He saith unto them, Go ye also into the vineyard; and whatsoever is right, *that* shall ye receive.

8 So when even was come, the lord of the vineyard saith unto his steward, Call the labourers, and give them *their* hire, beginning from the last unto the first.

9 And when they came that *were hired* about the eleventh hour, they received every man a penny.

10 But when the first came, they supposed that they should have received more; and they likewise received every man a penny.

11 And when they had received *it,* they murmured against the good man of the house.

12 Saying, These last have wrought *but* one hour, and thou hast made them equal unto us, which have borne the burden and heat of the day.

MATT. 20: 13-16

13 But he answered one of them, and said, Friend, I do thee no wrong: didst not thou agree with me for a penny?
14 Take *that* thine *is,* and go thy way: I will give unto this last, even as unto thee.
15 Is it not lawful for me to do what I will with mine own? is thine eye evil because I am good?

Right of contract established.

16 So that last shall be first, and the first last: for many be called, but few chosen.

LUKE 19: 1-11

Zaccheus meets Jesus.

AND *Jesus* entered and passed through Jericho.
2 And, behold, *there was* a man named Zaccheus, which was the chief among the publicans, and he was rich.
3 And he sought to see Jesus who he was; and could not for the press, because he was little of stature.
4 And he ran before, and climbed up into a sycamore-tree to see him; for he was to pass that *way.*
5 And, when Jesus came to the place, he looked up, and saw him, and said unto him, Zaccheus, make haste, and come down; for to-day I must abide at thy house.
6 And he made haste, and came down, and received him joyfully.
7 And when they saw *it,* they all murmured, saying, That he was gone to be guest with a man that is a sinner.

Zaccheus repents.

8 And Zaccheus stood, and said unto the Lord, Behold, Lord, the half of my goods I give to the poor; and if I have taken any thing from any man by false accusation, I restore him fourfold.
9 And Jesus said unto him, This day is salvation come to this house, forasmuch as he also is a son of Abraham.
10 For the Son of Man is come to seek and to save that which was lost.
11 And, as they heard these things, he added, and spake a parable, because he was nigh to Je-

LUKE 19: 12-23

rusalem, and because they thought that the kingdom of God should immediately appear.

The parable of the Pounds ("Minas" in Greek – silver coins)

12 He said, therefore, A certain nobleman went into a far country to receive for himself a kingdom, and to return.
13 And he called his ten servants, and delivered them ten pounds, and said unto them, Occupy till I come.
14 But his citizens hated him, and sent a message after him, saying, We will not have this *man* to reign over us.
15 And it came to pass, that when he returned, having received the kingdom, then he commanded these servants to be called unto him, to whom he had given the money, that he might know how much every man had gained by trading.
16 Then came the first, saying, Lord, thy pound hath gained ten pounds.
17 And he said unto him, Well, thou good servant; because thou hast been faithful in a very little, have thou authority over ten cities.

God desires profitable servants.

18 And the second came, saying, Lord thy pound hath gained five pounds.
19 And he said likewise to him, Be thou also over five cities.
20 And another came, saying, Lord, behold, *here is* thy pound, which I have kept laid up in a napkin:
21 For I feared thee, because thou art an austere man; thou takest up that thou layedst not down, and reapest that thou didst not sow.
22 And he saith unto him, Out of thine own mouth will I judge thee, *thou* wicked servant. Thou knewest that I was an austere man, taking up that I laid not down, and reaping that I did not sow:
23 Wherefore then gavest not thou my money into the bank, that at my coming I might have required mine own with usury?

Interest return legitimate in business.

LUKE 19: 24-28

24 And he said unto them that stood by, Take from him the pound, and give *it* to him that hath ten pounds.

25 (And they said unto him, Lord, he hath ten pounds.)

26 For I say unto you, That unto every one which hath, shall be given; and from him that hath not, even that he hath, shall be taken away from him.

27 But those mine enemies, which would not that I should reign over them, bring hither, and slay *them* before me.

28 And when he had thus spoken, he went before, ascending up to Jerusalem.

Jesus' triumphal entry into Jerusalem.

MATT. 21: 1-3

AND when they drew nigh unto Jerusalem, and were come to Bethpage, unto the mount of Olives, then sent Jesus two disciples,

2 Saying unto them, Go into the village over against you, and straightway ye shall find an ass tied, and a colt with her: loose *them*, and bring *them* unto me.

3 And if any *man* say aught unto you, ye shall say, The Lord hath need of them; and straightway he will send them.

MATT. 21: 6-8, 10

6 And the disciples went, and did as Jesus commanded them,

7 And brought the ass, and the colt, and put on them their clothes and set *him* thereon.

8 And a very great multitude spread their garments in the way; others cut down branches from the trees, and strawed them in the way.

10 And when he was come into Jerusalem, all the city was moved, saying, Who is this?

JOHN 12: 19, 20

19 The Pharisees, therefore, said among themselves, Perceive ye how ye prevail nothing? behold, the world is gone after him.

20 And there were certain Greeks among them, that came up to worship at the feast:

JOHN 12: 21-24

Jesus prophesies about the fruitfulness of His approaching death.

21 The same came, therefore, to Philip, which was of Bethsaida of Galilee, and desired him, saying, Sir, we would see Jesus.
22 Philip cometh and telleth Andrew; and again, Andrew and Philip tell Jesus.
23 And Jesus answered them, saying,
24 Verily, verily, I say unto you, Except a corn of wheat fall into the ground and die, it abideth alone: but if it die, it bringeth forth much fruit.

MATT. 21: 17

17 And he left them, and went out of the city into Bethany; and he lodged there.

MARK 11: 12, 15-19

The traders cast out from the temple.

12 And on the morrow, when they were come from Bethany,
15 Jesus went into the temple, and began to cast out them that sold and bought in the temple, and overthrew the tables of the money-changers, and the seats of them that sold doves;
16 And would not suffer that any man should carry *any* vessel through the temple.
17 And he taught, saying unto them, Is it not written, My house shall be called of all nations the house of prayer? but ye have made it a den of thieves.
18 And the scribes and chief priests heard *it,* and sought how they might destroy him: for they feared him, because all the people was astonished at his doctrine.
19 And when even was come, he went out of the city.

MARK 11: 27

27 And they come again to Jerusalem: and he was walking in the temple, there come to him the chief priests, and the scribes, and the elders,

MATT. 21: 28-31

Parable of the Two Sons.

28 And he said unto them, But what think ye? A *certain* man had two sons; and he came to the first, and said, Son go work to-day in my vineyard.
29 He answered and said, I will not: but afterward he repented and went.
30 And he came to the second and said likewise. And he answered and said, I *go,* sir: and went not.

Religious leaders identified with latter son.

31 Whether of them twain did the will of *his* father? They say unto him, The first. Jesus saith unto them, Verily I say unto you, That the publicans and the harlots go into the kingdom of God before you.

MATT. 21: 33/ MARK 12: 1-9

Parable of the Wicked Husbandmen.

33 Hear another parable: A *certain* man planted a vineyard, and set an hedge about *it,* and digged *a place for* the winefat, and built a tower, and let it out to husbandmen, and went into a far country.
2 And at the season he sent to the husbandmen a servant, that he might receive from the husbandmen of the fruit of the vineyard.
3 And they caught *him,* and beat him, and sent *him* away empty.
4 And again he sent unto them another servant; and at him they cast stones, and wounded *him* in the head, and sent *him* away shamefully handled.
5 And again he sent another; and him they killed, and many others; beating some, and killing some.
6 Having yet, therefore, one son, his wellbeloved, he sent him also last unto them, saying, They will reverence my son.
7 But those husbandmen said among themselves, This is the heir; come, let us kill him, and the inheritance shall be ours.
8 And they took him, and killed *him,* and cast *him* out of the vineyard.

Evil stewards will not inherit God's kingdom.

9 What shall, therefore, the lord of the vineyard do? he will come and destroy the husbandmen, and will give the vineyard unto others.

MATT. 21: 45, 46

45 And when the chief priests and Pharisees had heard his parables, they perceived that he spake of them.
46 But when they sought to lay hands on him, they feared the multitude, because they took him for a prophet.

MATT. 22: 1-3

Parable of the Wedding Feast.

AND Jesus answered, and spake unto them again by parables, and said,
2 The kingdom of heaven is like unto a certain king, which made a marriage for his son,
3 And sent forth his servants to call them that were bidden to the wedding; and they would not come.

MATT. 22: 4-14

4 Again, he sent forth other servants, saying, Tell them which are bidden, Behold, I have prepared my dinner: my oxen and *my* fatlings *are* killed, and all things *are* ready: come unto the marriage.
5 But they made light of *it,* and went their ways, one to his farm, another to his merchandise:
6 And the remnant took his servants, and intreated *them* spitefully, and slew *them.*
7 But when the king heard *thereof,* he was wroth: and he sent forth his armies, and destroyed those murderers, and burnt up their city.
8 Then saith he to his servants, The wedding is ready, but they which were bidden were not worthy.
9 Go ye therefore into the highways, and, as many as ye shall find, bid to the marriage.
10 So those servants went out into the highways, and gathered together all as many as they found, both bad and good: and the wedding was furnished with guests.
11 And when the king came in to see the guests, he saw there a man which had not on a wedding garment:
12 And he saith unto him, Friend, how camest thou in hither, not having a wedding garment? And he was speechless.
13 Then saith the king to the servants, Bind him hand and foot, and take him away; and cast *him* into outer darkness; there shall be weeping and gnashing of teeth.

Many called to God's work, but few choose to respond.

14 For many are called, but few *are* chosen.

MATT. 22: 15-18

Pharisees try to trick Jesus.

15 Then went the Pharisees, and took counsel how they might entangle him in *his* talk.
16 And they sent out unto him their disciples, with the herodians, saying, Master, we know that thou art true, and teachest the way of God in truth, neither carest thou for any *man:* for thou regardest not the person of men.
17 Tell us, therefore, What thinkest thou? Is it lawful to give tribute unto Cesar, or not?
18 But Jesus perceived their

wickedness, and said, Why tempt ye me, *ye* hypocrites?

MATT. 22: 19-33

19 Shew me the tribute-money. brought unto him a penny.

Jesus' answer: Render to Caesar his due, and to God His due.

20 And he saith unto them, Whose *is* this image and superscription?

21 They say unto him, Cesar's. Then saith he unto them, Render, therefore, unto Cesar the things which are Cesar's; and unto God the things that are God's.

22 When they heard *these words,* they marvelled, and left him, and went their way.

Sadducees question the Resurrection.

23 The same day came to him the Sadducees, which say that there is no resurrection, and asked him,

24 Saying, Master, Moses said, If a man die, having no children, his brother shall marry his wife, and raise up seed unto his brother.

25 Now, there were with us seven brethren: and the first, when he had married a wife, deceased; and having no issue, left his wife unto his brother:

26 Likewise, the second also, and the third, unto the seventh.

27 And last of all the woman died also.

28 Therefore, in the resurrection, whose wife shall she be of the seven? for they all had her.

29 Jesus answered, and said unto them, Ye do err, not knowing the scriptures, nor the power of God.

30 For in the resurrection they neither marry, nor are given in marriage; but are as the angels of God in heaven.

Jesus' answer: There is a Resurrection of the dead.

31 But as touching the resurrection of the dead, have ye not read that which was spoken unto you by God, saying,

32 I am the God of Abraham, and the God of Isaac, and the God of Jacob? God is not the God of the dead, but of the living.

33 And when the multitude heard *this,* they were astonished at his doctrine.

MARK 12: 28-31	28 And one of the scribes came, and having heard them reasoning together, and perceiving that he had answered them well, asked him, Which is the first commandment of all?	*The two greatest commandments:*
	29 And Jesus answered him, The first of all commandments *is,* Hear, O Israel; The Lord our God is one Lord:	*1. Love God with all your being.*
	30 And thou shalt love the Lord thy God with all thy heart, and with all thy soul, and with all thy mind, and with all thy strength. This *is* the first commandment.	
	31 And the second *is* like, *namely* this, Thou shalt love thy neighbour as thyself. There is none other commandment greater than these.	*2. Love your neighbor as yourself.*
MATT. 22: 40	40 On these two commandments hang all the law and the prophets.	
MARK 12: 32, 33	32 And the scribe said unto him, Well, Master, thou hast said the truth: for there is one God; and there is none other but he:	
	33 And to love him with all the heart, and with all the understanding, and with all the soul, and with all the strength, and to love *his* neighbour as himself, is more than all whole burnt-offerings and sacrifices.	
MATT. 23: 1-6	THEN spake Jesus to the multitude, and to his disciples	*Precepts drawn from evil examples of the scribes and Pharisees:*
	2 Saying, The scribes and the Pharisees sit in Moses' seat:	
	3 All therefore whatsoever they bid you observe, *that* observe and do; but do not ye after their works: for they say and do not.	*Hypocrisy is wrong.*
	4 For they bind heavy burdens and grievous to be borne, and lay *them* on mens' shoulders; but they *themselves* will not move them with one of their fingers.	
	5 But all their works they do for to be seen of men: they make broad their phylacteries, and enlarge the borders of their garments.	*Vanity is short-sighted.*
	6 And love the uppermost rooms at feasts, and the chief seats in the synagogues.	

MATT. 23: 7-19

7 And greetings in the markets, and to be called of men, Rabbi, Rabbi.
8 But be not ye called Rabbi; for one is your Master, *even* Christ; and all ye are brethren.
9 And call no *man* your Father upon the earth: for one is your Father, which is in heaven.
10 Neither be ye called masters: for one is your master, *even* Christ.

A person who serves is greatest in God's eyes.

11 But he that is greatest among you shall be your servant.
12 And whosoever shall exalt himself shall be abased; and he that shall humble himself shall be exalted.

Humility brings exaltation.

13 But woe unto you, scribes and Pharisees, hypocrites! for ye shut up the kingdom of heaven against men: for ye neither go in *your selves;* neither suffer ye them that are entering, to go in.
14 Woe unto you, scribes and Pharisees, hypocrites! for ye devour widows' houses, and for a pretence make long prayer: therefore ye shall receive the greater damnation.
15 Woe unto you, scribes and Pharisees, hypocrites! for ye compass sea and land to make one proselyte; and when he is made, ye make him two-fold more the child of hell than yourselves.
16 Woe unto you, *ye* blind guides! which say, Whosoever shall swear by the temple, it is nothing; but whosoever shall swear by the gold of the temple, he is a debtor.
17 *Ye* fools and blind! for whether *is* greater, the gold, or the temple that sanctifieth the gold?
18 And, whosoever shall swear by the altar, it is nothing; but whosoever sweareth by the gift that is upon it, he is guilty.
19 *Ye* fools, and blind! for whether *is* greater, the gift, or the altar that sanctifieth the gift?

MATT. 23: 20-33

Precepts (continued)

20 Whoso, therefore, shall swear by the altar, sweareth by it, and by all things thereon.

21 And whoso shall swear by the temple, sweareth by it, and by him that dwelleth therein.

22 And he that shall swear by heaven, sweareth by the throne of God, and by him that sitteth thereon.

Don't be legalistic and forget justice, mercy, and faith.

23 Woe unto you, scribes and Pharisees, hypocrites! for ye pay tithe of mint, and anise, and cummin, and have omitted the weightier *matters* of the law, judgment, mercy, and faith: these ought ye to have done, and not to leave the other undone.

24 *Ye* blind guides! which strain at a gnat, and swallow a camel.

25 Woe unto you, scribes and Pharisees, hypocrites! for ye make clean the outside of the cup and of the platter, but within they are full of extortion and excess.

26 *Thou* blind Pharisee. cleanse first that *which* is within the cup and platter, that the outside of them may be clean also.

Outward appearances can be deceiving.

27 Woe unto you, scribes and Pharisees, hypocrites! for ye are like unto whited sepulchres, which indeed appear beautiful outward, but are within full of dead *mens'* bones, and of all uncleanness.

28 Even so ye also outwardly appear righteous unto men, but within ye are full of hypocrisy and iniquity.

29 Woe unto you, scribes and Pharisees, hypocrites! because ye build the tombs of the prophets, and garnish the sepulchres of the righteous,

30 And say, If we had been in the days of our fathers, we would not have been partakers with them in the blood of the prophets.

31 Wherefore ye be witnesses unto yourselves, that ye are the children of them which killed the prophets.

32 Fill ye up then the measure of your fathers.

33 *Ye* serpents, *ye* generation of vipers! how can ye escape the damnation of hell?

MARK 12: 41-44	41 And Jesus sat over against the treasury, and beheld how the people cast money into the treasury: and many that were rich cast in much. 42 And there came a certain poor widow, and she threw in two mites, which make a farthing. 43 And he called *unto him* his disciples, and saith unto them, Verily I say unto you, That this poor widow hath cast more in than all they which have cast into the treasury:	*The widow's two mites (coins).*
	44 For all *they* did cast in of their abundance; but she of her want did cast in all that she had, *even* all her living.	*She gave her all.*
MATT. 24: 1, 2	AND Jesus went out, and departed from the temple; and his disciples came *to him*, for to shew him the buildings of the temple. 2 And Jesus said unto them, See ye not all these things? Verily I say unto you, There shall not be left here one stone upon another, that shall not be thrown down.	*Jesus predicts the destruction of the temple. . .*
MATT. 24: 16-21	16 Then let them which be in Judea flee into the mountains: 17 Let him which is on the house-top not come down to take any thing out of his house: 18 Neither let him which is in the field return back to take his clothes. 19 And woe unto them that are with child, and to them that give suck in those days! 20 But pray ye that your flight be not in the winter, neither on the sabbath-day:	
	21 For then shall be great tribulation, such as was not since the beginning of the world to this time, no, nor ever shall be.	*...and a great tribulation.*
MATT. 24: 29	29 Immediately after the tribulation of those days shall the sun be darkened, and the moon shall not give her light, and the stars shall fall from heaven, and the powers of the heavens shall be shaken:	

MATT. 24: 32, 33	32 Now learn a parable of the fig-tree; When his branch is yet tender, and putteth forth leaves, ye know that summer *is* nigh: 33 So likewise ye, when ye shall see all these things, know that it is near, *even* at the doors.	*Parable of the Fig Tree.*
MATT. 24: 36-44	36 But of that day and hour knoweth no *man;* no, not the angels of heaven, but my Father only. 37 But as the days of Noe *were,* so shall also the coming of the Son of Man be. 38 For as in the days that were before the flood they were eating and drinking, marrying and giving in marriage, until the day that Noe entered into the ark, 39 And knew not until the flood came, and took them all away; 40 Then shall two be in the field, the one shall be taken, and the other left. 41 Two *women shall be* grinding at the mill; the one shall be taken, and the other left.	*No one knows the day or hour of Jesus' (Son of Man's) return.*
	42 Watch, therefore; for ye know not what hour your Lord doth come. 43 But know this, that if the good man of the house had known in what watch the thief would come, he would have watched, and would not have suffered his house to be broken up. 44 Therefore be ye also ready:	*Watch, be ready.*
MATT. 24: 45-49	45 Who then is a faithful and wise servant, whom his lord hath made ruler over his household, to give them meat in due season? 46 Blessed *is* that servant, whom his lord, when he cometh, shall find so doing. 47 Verily I say unto you, That he shall make him ruler over all his goods. 48 But and if that evil servant shall say in his heart, My lord delayeth his coming; 49 And shall begin to smite *his* fellow-servants, and to eat and drink with the drunken;	*The faithful and wise servant will be blessed.*

MATT. 24: 50, 51	50 The lord of that servant shall come in a day when he looketh not for *him*, and in an hour that he is not aware of. 51 And shall cut him asunder and appoint *him* his portion with the hypocrites: there shall be weeping and gnashing of teeth.	*The evil servant will be punished.*
MATT. 25: 1-13	THEN shall the kingdom of heaven be likened unto ten virgins, which took their lamps, and went forth to meet the bridegroom. 2 And five of them were wise, and five *were* foolish.	*Parable of the Wise and Foolish Virgins.*
	3 They that *were* foolish took their lamps, and took no oil with them: 4 But the wise took oil in their vessels with their lamps. 5 While the bridegroom tarried, they all slumbered and slept. 6 And at midnight there was a cry made, Behold, the bridegroom cometh; go ye out to meet him. 7 Then all those virgins arose, and trimmed their lamps. 8 And the foolish said unto the wise, Give us of your oil, for our lamps are gone out. 9 But the wise answered, saying, *Not so:* lest there be not enough for us and you: but go ye rather to them that sell, and buy for yourselves.	*Foolish virgins unprepared.*
	10 And while they went to buy, the bridegroom came; and they that were ready went in with him to the marriage: and the door was shut. 11 Afterward came also the other virgins, saying, Lord, Lord, open to us. 12 But he answered and said, Verily I say unto you, I know you not. 13 Watch, therefore,	*Wise virgins prepared.*
MATT. 25: 14, 15	14 For *the kingdom of heaven is* as a man travelling into a far country, *who* called his own servants, and delivered unto them his goods. 15 And unto one he gave five talents, to another two, and to	*Parable of the Talents (silver money).*

MATT. 25: 16-26

another one; to every man according to his several ability; and straightway took his journey.

Servant's rates of return:

16 Then he that had received the five talents went and traded with the same, and made *them* other five talents. *100%*

17 And likewise he that *had received* two, he also gained other two. *100%*

18 But he that had received one, went and digged in the earth, and hid his lord's money. *0%*

19 After a long time the lord of those servants cometh, and reckoneth with them.

20 And so he that had received five talents came, and brought other five talents, saying, Lord, thou deliveredst unto me five talents: behold, I have gained beside them five talents more.

21 His lord said unto him, Well done, *thou* good and faithful servant: thou hast been faithful over a few things, I will make thee ruler over many things: enter thou into the joy of thy lord.

Profitable servants rewarded.

22 He also that had received two talents came, and said, Lord, thou deliveredst unto me two talents: behold, I have gained two other talents beside them.

23 His lord said unto him, Well done, good and faithful servant: thou hast been faithful over a few things, I will make thee ruler over many things: enter thou into the joy of thy lord.

24 Then he which had received the one talent came, and said, Lord, I knew thee, that thou art an hard man, reaping where thou hast not sown, and gathering where thou hast not strawed:

25 And I was afraid, and went and hid thy talent in the earth: lo, *there* thou hast *that is* thine.

26 His lord answered, and said unto him, *Thou* wicked and slothful servant, thou knewest that I reap where I sowed not, and gather where I have not strawed:

MATT. 25: 27-30

27 Thou oughtest, therefore, to have put my money to the exchangers, and *then* at my coming I should have received mine own with usury.

Profitable servants given greater responsibility.

28 Take, therefore, the talent from him, and give it unto him which hath ten talents.

29 For unto every one that hath shall be given, and he shall have abundance: but from him that hath not, shall be taken away even that which he hath.

30 And cast ye the unprofitable servant into outer darkness: there shall be weeping and gnashing of teeth.

LUKE 21: 34-36

Unprofitable servant punished.

34 And take heed to yourselves, lest at any time your hearts be overcharged with surfeiting, and drunkenness, and cares of this life, and *so* that day come upon you unawares.

35 For as a snare shall it come on all them that dwell on the face of the whole earth.

36 Watch ye, therefore, and pray always, that ye may be accounted worthy to escape all these things that shall come to pass, and to stand before the Son of Man.

MATT. 25: 31-36

Judgment at Jesus' return.

31 When the Son of Man shall come in his glory, and all the holy angels with him, then shall he sit upon the throne of his glory:

Parable of the Sheep and Goats

32 And before him shall be gathered all nations: and he shall separate them one from another, as a shepherd divideth his sheep from the goats:

33 And he shall set the sheep on his right hand, but the goats on the left.

Eternal life for those who love their neighbors.

34 Then shall the King say unto them on his right hand, Come, ye blessed of my Father, inherit the kingdom prepared for you from the foundation of the world:

35 For I was an hungered, and ye gave me meat: I was thirsty, and ye gave me drink: I was a stranger, and ye took me in:

36 Naked, and ye clothed me: I was sick, and ye visited me: I was in prison, and ye came unto me.

MATT. 25: 37-46

37 Then shall the righteous answer him, saying, Lord, when saw we thee an hungered, and fed *thee?* or thirsty, and gave *thee* drink?

38 When saw we thee a stranger, and took *thee* in? or naked, and clothed *thee?*

39 Or when saw we thee sick, or in prison, and came unto *thee?*

40 And the King shall answer, and say unto them, Verily I say unto you, Inasmuch as ye have done *it* unto one of the least of these my brothren, ye have done *it* unto me.

Death for those who do not love their neighbors.

41 Then shall he say also unto them on the left hand, Depart from me, ye cursed, into everlasting fire, prepared for the devil and his angels;

42 For I was an hungered, and ye gave me no meat: I was thirsty, and ye gave me no drink:

43 I was a stranger, and ye took me not in: naked, and ye clothed me not: sick, and in prison, and ye visited me not.

44 Then shall they also answer him, saying, Lord, when saw we *thee* an hungered, or athirst, or a stranger, or naked, or sick, or in prison, and did not minister unto thee?

45 Then shall he answer them, saying, Verily I say unto you, Inasmuch as ye did *it* not to one of the least of these, ye did *it* not to me.

46 And these shall go away into everlasting punishment: but the righteous into life eternal.

MARK 14: 1-3

A plot to kill Jesus.

AFTER two days was *the feast of* the passover, and of unleavened bread: and the chief priests and the scribes sought how they might take him by craft, and put *him* to death.

2 But they said, Not on the feast-*day*, lest there be an uproar of the people.

3 And being in Bethany, in the house of Simon the leper, as he sat at meat, there came a woman,

MARK 14: 4-8	having an alabaster-box of ointment of spikenard, very precious; and she brake the box, and poured *it* on his head. 4 And there were some that had indignation within themselves, and said, Why was this waste of the ointment made? 5 For it might have been sold for more than three hundred pence, and have been given to the poor. And they murmured against her. 6 And Jesus said, Let her alone, why trouble ye her? she hath wrought a good work on me. 7 For ye have the poor with you always, and whensoever ye will, ye may do them good; but me ye have not always. 8 She hath done what she could; she is come aforehand to anoint my body to the burying.	*A woman anoints Jesus: a worthwhile expenditure.*
MATT. 26: 14-16	14 Then one of the twelve called Judas Iscariot, went unto the chief priests, 15 And said *unto them,* What will ye give me, and I will deliver him unto you? And they covenanted with him for thirty pieces of silver. 16 And from that time he sought opportunity to betray him.	*Judas undertakes to betray Jesus.*
MATT. 26: 17-20	17 Now, the first *day* of the *feast of* unleavened bread, the disciples came to Jesus, saying unto him, Where wilt thou that we prepare for thee to eat the passover? 18 And he said, Go into the city to such a man and say unto him, The Master saith, My time is at hand; I will keep the passover at thy house with my disciples. 19 And the disciples did as Jesus had appointed them; and they made ready the passover. 20 Now, when the even was come, he sat down with the twelve.	*Passover prepared.*
LUKE 22: 24, 25	24 And there was also a strife among them, which of them should be accounted the greatest. 25 And he said unto them, The kings of the Gentiles exercise lordship over them; and they that exercise authority upon them are called benefactors.	*Don't exercise authority as Gentile kings.*

LUKE 22: 26, 27	26 But ye *shall* not *be* so: but he that is greatest among you, let him be as the younger; and he that is chief, as he that doth serve. 27 For whether *is* greater, he that sitteth at meat, or he that serveth? *is* not he that sitteth at meat? but I am among you as he that serveth.	*Follow Jesus' example of service.*
JOHN 13: 2, 4-17	2 And supper being ended, 4 He riseth from supper, and laid aside his garments; and took a towel, and girded himself. 5 After that he poureth water into a bason, and began to wash the disciples' feet, and to wipe them with the towel wherewith he was girded. 6 Then cometh he to Simon Peter: and Peter saith unto him, Lord, dost thou wash my feet? 7 Jesus answered, and said unto him, What I do, thou knowest not now; but thou shalt know hereafter. 8 Peter saith unto him, Thou shalt never wash my feet. Jesus answered him, If I wash thee not, thou hast no part with me. 9 Simon Peter saith unto him, Lord, not my feet only, but also *my* hands and *my* head.	*Jesus washes His disciples feet: master becomes the servant.*
	10 Jesus saith to him, He that is washed, needeth not, save to wash *his* feet, but is clean every whit: and ye are clean, but not all. 11 For he knew who should betray him; therefore said he, Ye are not all clean. 12 So, after he had washed their feet, and had taken his garments, and was set down again, he said unto them, Know ye what I have done to you? 13 Ye call me Master and Lord: and ye say well; for *so* I am. 14 If I then, *your* Lord and Master, have washed your feet, ye also ought to wash one another's feet.	*Judas not clean.*
	15 For I have given you an example, that ye should do as I have done to you. 16 Verily, verily, I say unto you, The servant is not greater than his lord: neither he that is sent, greater than he that sent him. 17 If ye know these things, happy are ye if ye do them.	*Jesus exhorts to follow His example.*

JOHN 13: 21-26, 31, 34, 35

21 When Jesus had thus said, he was troubled in spirit, and testified, and said, Verily, verily, I say unto you, that one of you shall betray me.

Jesus troubled of mind.

22 Then the disciples looked one on another, doubting of whom he spake.
23 Now there was leaning on Jesus' bosom one of his disciples, whom Jesus loved.
24 Simon Peter, therefore, beckoned to him, that he should ask who it should be of whom he spake.
25 He then, lying on Jesus' breast, saith unto him, Lord, who is it?
26 Jesus answered, He it is, to whom I shall give a sop, when I have dipped *it.* And when he had dipped the sop, he gave *it* to Judas Iscariot, *the son* of Simon.
31 Therefore, when he was gone out, Jesus said,
34 A new commandment I give unto you, That ye love one another; as I have loved you, that ye also love one another.

Sign that identifies Christians: loving one another.

35 By this shall all *men* know that ye are my disciples, if ye have love one to another.

MATT. 26: 31, 33

31 Then saith Jesus unto them, All ye shall be offended because of me this night:
33 Peter answered, and said unto him, Though all *men* shall be offended because of thee, *yet* will I never be offended.

LUKE 22: 33, 34

33 I am ready to go with thee, both into prison, and to death.

Jesus predicts Peter's denial.

34 And he said, I tell thee, Peter, the cock shall not crow this day, before that thou shalt thrice deny that thou knowest me.

MATT. 26: 35, 36

35 Peter said unto him, Though I should die with thee, yet will I not deny thee. Likewise also said all the disciples.
36 Then cometh Jesus with them unto a place called Gethsemane, and saith unto the disciples, Sit ye here, while I go and pray yonder.

MATT. 26: 37-45	37 And he took with him Peter and the two sons of Zebedee, and began to be sorrowful and very heavy. 38 Then saith he unto them, My soul is exceedingly sorrowful, even unto death: tarry ye here, and watch with me. 39 And he went a little farther, and fell on his face, and prayed, saying, O my Father, if it be possible, let this cup pass from me: nevertheless, not as I will, but as thou *wilt*.	*Jesus prays in the Garden.*
	40 And he cometh unto the disciples, and findeth them asleep, and saith unto Peter, What! could ye not watch with me one hour? 41 Watch and pray, that ye enter not into temptation: the spirit indeed *is* willing, but the flesh *is* weak.	*Disciples too tired to watch.*
	42 He went away again the second time, and prayed, saying, O my Father, if this cup may not pass away from me, except I drink it, thy will be done. 43 And he came and found them asleep again: for their eyes were heavy. 44 And he left them, and went away again, and prayed the third time, saying the same words. 45 Then cometh he to his disciples, and saith unto them, Sleep on now, and take *your* rest:	*Jesus accepts His Father's will.*
JOHN 18: 1-3	WHEN Jesus had spoken these words, he went forth with his disciples over the brook Cedron, where was a garden, into which he entered, and his disciples. 2 And Judas also, which betrayed him, knew the place: for Jesus oft-times resorted thither with his disciples. 3 Judas then, having received a band *of men* and officers from the chief priests and Pharisees, cometh thither with lanterns, and torches, and weapons.	*Judas conducts the officers to Jesus.*

MATT. 26: 48-50	48 Now he that betrayed him gave them a sign, saying, Whomsoever I shall kiss, that same is he: hold him fast. 49 And forthwith he came to Jesus, and said, Hail, Master, and kissed him. 50 And Jesus said unto him, Friend, wherefore art thou come?	*Betrayal sign: a kiss.*
JOHN 18: 4-8	4 Jesus, therefore, knowing all things that should come upon him, went forth, and said unto them, Whom seek ye? 5 They answered him, Jesus of Nazareth. Jesus saith unto them, I am *he.* (And Judas also, which betrayed him, stood with them.) 6 As soon then as he had said unto them, I am *he,* they went backward, and fell to the ground. 7 Then asked he them again, Whom seek ye? And they said, Jesus of Nazareth. 8 Jesus answered, I have told you, that I am *he:* if, therefore, ye seek me, let these go their way;	*Jesus is arrested.*
MATT. 26: 50-52, 55, 56	50 Then came they and laid hands on Jesus, and took him. 51 And, behold, one of them, which were with Jesus, stretched out *his* hand, and drew his sword, and struck a servant of the high priest, and smote off his ear. 52 Then said Jesus unto him, Put up again thy sword into his place: for all they that take the sword shall perish with the sword. 55 In that same hour said Jesus to the Are ye come out as against a thief, with swords, and staves for to take me? I sat daily with you teaching in the temple, and ye laid no hold on me. 56 Then all the disciples forsook him and fled.	*Peter attempts to defend Jesus.* *Disciples flee.*
MARK 14: 51, 52	51 And there followed him a certain young man, having a linen cloth cast about *his* naked *body;* and the young men laid hold on him: 52 And he left the linen cloth, and fled from them naked.	*Mark escapes naked.*

MATT. 26: 57

57 And they that had laid hold on Jesus, led *him* away to Caiaphas the high priest, where the scribes and the elders were assembled.

Jesus led away to the chief priests.

JOHN 18: 15, 16, 18, 17

15 And Simon Peter followed Jesus, and *so did* another disciple. That disciple was known unto the high priest, and went in with Jesus into the palace of the high priest.

16 But Peter stood at the door without. Then went out that other disciple, which was known unto the high priest, and spake unto her that kept the door, and brought in Peter.

18 And the servants and officers stood there, who had made a fire of coals, (for it was cold,) and they warmed themselves: and Peter stood with them, and warmed himself.

17 Then saith the damsel, that kept the door, unto Peter, Art not thou also *one* of this man's disciples? He saith, I am not.

Peter denies being one of Jesus' disciples three times, as predicted.

JOHN 18: 25-27

25 And Simon Peter stood and warmed himself: they said, therefore, unto him, Art not thou also *one* of his disciples? He denied *it,* and said, I am not.

26 One of the servants of the high priest, (being *his* kinsman whose ear Peter cut off,) saith, Did not I see thee in the garden with him?

27 Peter then denied again; and immediately the cock crew.

MATT. 26: 75

75 And Peter remembered the words of Jesus, which said unto him, Before the cock crow, thou shalt deny me thrice. And he went out, and wept bitterly.

JOHN 18: 19, 20

19 The high priest then asked Jesus of his disciples, and of his doctrine.

20 Jesus answered him, I spake openly to the world; I ever taught in the synagogue, and in the temple, whither the Jews always resort; and in secret I have said nothing.

Jesus questioned about His doctrine by Caiaphas.

JOHN 18: 21-23

21 Why askest thou me? ask them which heard me, what I have said unto them: behold, they know what I said.

22 And, when he had thus spoken, one of the officers which stood by struck Jesus with the palm of his hand, saying, Answerest thou the high priest so?

Officer strikes Jesus for His response.

23 Jesus answered him, If I have spoken evil, bear witness of the evil; but if well, why smitest thou me?

MARK 14: 53, 55-61

53 And they led Jesus away to the high priest; and with him were assembled all the chief priests, and the elders, and the scribes.

Sanhedrin seeks witnesses against Jesus.

55 And the chief priests, and all the council, sought for witness against Jesus to put him to death; and found none:

56 For many bare false witness against him, but their witness agreed not together.

57 And there arose certain, and bare false witness against him, saying,

58 We heard him say, I will destroy this temple that is made with hands, and within three days I will build another made without hands.

59 But neither so did their witness agree together.

Witnesses' testimonies do not agree.

60 And the high priest stood up in the midst, and asked Jesus, saying, Answerest thou nothing? what *is it which* these witnesses against thee.

61 But he held his peace, and answered nothing. Again the high priest asked him, and said unto him, Art thou the Christ, the Son of the Blessed?

LUKE 22: 67, 68, 70

67 And he said unto them, If I tell you, ye will not believe:

68 And if I also ask *you,* ye will not answer me, nor let *me* go.

70 Then said they all, Art thou then the Son of God? And he said unto them, Ye say that I am.

MARK 14: 63, 64

63 Then the high priest rent his clothes, and saith, What need we any further witnesses?

They condemn Him to death . . .

64 Ye have heard the blasphemy: what think ye? And they

MARK 14: 65	all condemned him to be guilty of death. 65 And some began to spit on him, and to cover his face, and to buffet him, and say unto him, Prophesy: and the servants did strike him with the palms of their hands.	*...and beat Him.*
JOHN 18: 28-31, 33-38	28 Then led they Jesus from Caiaphas unto the hall of judgement, and it was early; and they themselves went not into the judgment-hall, lest they should be defiled; but that they might eat the passover.	*Jesus arraigned before Pilate.*
	29 Pilate then went out unto them, and said, What accusation bring ye against this man?	
	30 They answered, and said unto him, If he were not a malefactor, we would not have delivered him up unto thee.	
	31 Then said Pilate unto them, Take ye him, and judge him according to your law. The Jews, therefore, said unto him, It is not lawful for us to put any man to death;	
	33 Then Pilate entered into the judgment-hall again, and called Jesus, and said unto him, Art thou the King of the Jews?	
	34 Jesus answered him, Sayest thou this thing of thyself, or did others tell it thee of me?	
	35 Pilate answered, Am I a Jew? Thine own nation and the chief priests have delivered thee unto me. What hast thou done?	
	36 Jesus answered, My kingdom is not of this world. If my kingdom were of this world, then would my servants fight, that I should not be delivered to the Jews: but now is my kingdom not from hence.	
	37 Pilate, therefore, said unto him, Art thou a King then? Jesus answered, thou sayest that I am a king. To this end was I born, and for this cause came I into the world, that I should bear witness unto the truth. Every one that is of the truth heareth my voice.	*Jesus announces His destiny – to be a King.*
	38 Pilate saith unto him, What is truth? And when he had said this, he went out again unto the Jews, and saith unto them, I find in him no fault *at all.*	*Pilate finds no fault.*

LUKE 23: 5

5 And they were the more fierce, saying, He stirreth up the people, teaching throughout all Jewry, beginning from Galilee to this place.

MATT. 27: 13

13 Then said Pilate unto him, Hearest thou not how many things they witness against thee?

LUKE 23: 6-12

Pilate sends Jesus to face Herod.

6 When Pilate heard of Galilee, he asked whether the man were a Galilean.

7 And as soon as he knew that he belonged unto Herod's jurisdiction, he sent him to Herod, who himself also was at Jerusalem at that time.

8 And when Herod saw Jesus, he was exceeding glad: for he was desirous to see him of a long *season*, because he had heard many things of him; and he hoped to have seen some miracle done by him.

Jesus remains silent.

9 Then he questioned with him in many words; but he answered him nothing.

10 And the chief priests and scribes stood, and vehemently accused him.

Returned to Pilate.

11 And Herod, with his men of war, set him at nought, and mocked *him,* and arrayed him in a gorgeous robe, and sent him again to Pilate.

12 And the same day Pilate and Herod were made friends together: for before they were at enmity between themselves.

LUKE 23: 13-16

13 And Pilate, when he had called together the chief priests, and the rulers, and the people,

Neither Pilate nor Herod find fault.

14 Said unto them, Ye have brought this man unto me, as one that perverteth the people; and, behold, I, having examined *him* before you, have found no fault in this man, touching those things whereof ye accuse him:

15 No, nor yet Herod: for I sent you to him; and, lo, nothing worthy of death is done unto him;

16 I will, therefore, chastise him, and release *him.*

MATT. 27: 15-23, 26

15 Now at *that* feast the governor was wont to release unto the people a prisoner, whom they would.

16 And they had then a notable prisoner, called Barabbas.

Jesus takes the place of Barabbas.

17 Therefore, when they were gathered together, Pilate said unto them, Whom will ye that I release unto you? Barabbas, or Jesus, which is called Christ?

18 For he knew that for envy they had delivered him.

19 When he was set down on the judgment-seat, his wife sent unto him, saying, Have thou nothing to do with that just man: for I have suffered many things this day in a dream because of him.

20 But the chief priests and elders persuaded the multitude that they should ask Barabbas, and destroy Jesus.

21 The governor answered, and said unto them, Whether of the twain will ye that I release unto you? They said, Barabbas.

22 Pilate saith unto them, What shall I do then with Jesus, which is called Christ? *They* all say unto him, Let him be crucified.

Multitude calls for His crucification.

23 And the governor said, Why, what evil hath he done? But they cried out the more, saying, Let him be crucified.

26 Then released he Barabbas, unto them; and when he had scourged Jesus, he delivered *him* to be crucified.

Jesus scourged and delivered to be crucified.

MATT. 27: 27, 29-31

27 Then the soldiers of the governor took Jesus into the common hall, and gathered unto him and the whole band *of soldiers.*

29 And when they had platted a crown of thorns, they put *it* upon his head, and a reed in his right hand; and they bowed the knee before him, and mocked him, saying, Hail, king of the Jews!

Soldiers mock Jesus.

30 And they spit upon him, and took the reed, and smote him on the head.

31 And after that they had mocked him, they took the robe off from him, and put his own raiment on him, and led him away to crucify *him.*

MATT. 27: 3-8

3 Then Judas which had betrayed him, when he saw that he was condemned, repented himself, and brought again the thirty pieces of silver to the chief priests and elders,

4 Saying, I have sinned, in that I have betrayed the innocent blood. And they said, What *is that* to us? see thou *to that.*

Judas hangs himself.

5 And he cast down the pieces of silver in the temple, and departed, and went and hanged himself.

6 And the chief priests took the silver pieces, and said, It is not lawful for to put them into the treasury, because it is the price of blood.

7 And they took counsel, and bought with them the potter's field, to bury strangers in.

8 Wherefore that field was called, The field of blood, unto his day.

LUKE 23: 26-32

26 And, as they led him away, they laid hold upon one Simon, a Cyrenian, coming out of the country, and on him they laid the cross, that he might bear *it* after Jesus.

27 And there followed him a great company of people, and of women, which also bewailed and lamented him.

Jesus foretells of Jerusalem's destruction.

28 But Jesus, turning unto them, said, Daughters of Jerusalem, weep not for me, but weep for yourselves, and for your children.

29 For, behold, the days are coming, in which they shall say, Blessed *are* the barren, and the wombs that never bare, and the paps which never gave suck.

30 Then shall they begin to say to the mountains, Fall on us; and to the hills, Cover us.

31 For if they do these things in a green tree, what shall be done in the dry?

32 And there were also two others, malefactors, led with him to be put to death.

JOHN 19: 17-24

17 And he, bearing his cross, went forth into a place called *the place* of a skull, which is called in the Hebrew, Golgotha;

Jesus crucified with two others at Golgotha.

18 Where they crucified him, and two others with him, on either side one, and Jesus in the midst.

19 And Pilate wrote a title, and put it on the cross. And the writing was, JESUS OF NAZARETH, THE KING OF THE JEWS.

Pilate places a title on the cross in three languages.

20 This title then read many of the Jews: for the place where Jesus was crucified was nigh to the city: and it was written in Hebrew, *and* Greek, *and* Latin.

21 Then said the chief priests of the Jews to Pilate, Write not, The King of the Jews; but that he said, I am King of the Jews.

22 Pilate answered, What I have written, I have written.

23 Then the soldiers, when they had crucified Jesus, took his garments, and made four parts, to every soldier a part, and also *his* coat: now the coat was without seam, woven from the top throughout.

Soldiers cast lots for Jesus' garments.

24 They said, therefore, among themselves, Let us not rend it, but cast lots for it, whose it shall be:

MATT. 27: 39-43

39 And they that passed by reviled him, wagging their heads,

Jesus reviled and mocked.

40 And saying, Thou that destroyest the temple, and buildest *it* in three days, save thyself. If thou be the Son of God, come down from the cross.

41 Likewise also the chief priests mocking *him*, with the scribes and elders, said,

42 He saved others; himself he cannot save. If he be the King of Israel, let him now come down from the cross, and we will believe him.

43 He trusted in God; let him deliver him now, if he will have him: for he said, I am the Son of God.

LUKE 23:
39-41, 34

One criminal rebukes the other.

39 And one of the malefactors, which were hanged, railed on him, saying, If thou be Christ, save thyself and us.
40 But the other, answering, rebuked him, saying, Dost not thou fear God, seeing thou art in the same condemnation?
41 And we indeed justly; for we receive the due reward of our deeds: but this man hath done nothing amiss.

Jesus forgives His enemies.

34 Then said Jesus, Father, forgive them; for they know not what they do.

JOHN 19:
25-27

25 Now there stood by the cross of Jesus, his mother, and his mother's sister, Mary, the *wife* of Cleophas, and Mary Magdalene.
26 When Jesus, therefore, saw his mother, and the disciple standing by whom he Woman, behold thy Son!
27 Then saith he to the disciple, Behold thy mother! And from that hour that disciple took her unto his own *home.*

MATT. 27:
46-50, 55-56

Jesus cries out when speared in His side.

46 And about the ninth hour, Jesus cried with a loud voice, saying, Eli, Eli, lama sabachthani? that is to say, My God, my God, why hast thou forsaken me?
47 Some of them that stood there, when they heard *that,* said, This *man* calleth for Elias.
48 And straightway one of them ran, and took a spunge, and filled *it* with vinegar, and put *it* on a reed, and gave him to drink.
49 The rest said, Let be, let us see whether Elias will come to save him.

Jesus dies.

50 Jesus, when he had cried again with a loud voice, yielded up the ghost.
55 And many women were there, beholding afar off, which followed Jesus from Galilee, ministering unto him:
56 Among which was Mary Magdalene, and Mary the mother of James and Joses, and the mother of Zebedee's children.

JOHN 19: 31-34, 38-42	31 The Jews, therefore, because it was the preparation, that the bodies should not remain upon the cross on the sabbath-day, (for that sabbath-day was an high day,) besought Pilate that their legs might be broken, and *that* they might be taken away.	*Jesus' body removed from the cross before a high day sabbath. [Annual sabbath rather than weekly sabbath].*
	32 Then came the soldiers, and brake the legs of the first, and of the other which was crucified with him.	
	33 But when they came to Jesus, and saw that he was dead already, they brake not his legs:	
	34 But one of the soldiers with a spear pierced his side, and forthwith came thereout blood and water.	
	38 And after this, Joseph of Arimathea, (being a disciple of Jesus, but secretly for fear of the Jews,) besought Pilate that he might take away the body of Jesus: and Pilate gave*him* leave. He came therefore, and took the body of Jesus.	*Joseph of Arimathea obtains the body of Jesus.*
	39 And there came also Nicodemus, (which at the first came to Jesus by night) and brought a mixture of myrrh and aloes, about an hundred pound *weight*,	
	40 Then took they the body of Jesus, and wound it in linen clothes with the spices as the manner of the Jews is to bury.	
	41 Now, in the place where he was crucified, there was a garden; and in the garden a new sepulchre, wherein was never man yet laid.	
	42 There laid they Jesus,	*Jesus buried in Joseph's tomb.*
MATT. 27: 60	60 and rolled a great stone to the door of the sepulchre, and departed.	

APPENDIX I

Jefferson's Syllabus, originally written by him in 1803, is reprinted here exactly as it appeared in the "Introduction" to the first ever, private edition by N.D. Thompson Co. in 1902.

SYLLABUS OF AN ESTIMATE OF THE DOCTRINES OF JESUS, COMPARED WITH THOSE OF OTHERS.

In a comparative view of the ethics of the enlightened nations of antiquity, of the Jews, and of Jesus, no notice should be taken of the corruptions of reason among the ancients, to wit, the idolatry and superstition of the vulgar, nor of the corruptions of Christianity by the learned among its professors. Let a just view be taken of the moral principles inculcated by the most esteemed of the sects of ancient philosophy, or of their individuals; particularly Pythagoras, Socrates, Epicurus, Cicero, Epictetus, Seneca, Antoninus.

I. PHILOSOPHERS.

1. Their precepts related chiefly to ourselves, and the government of those passions which, unrestrained, would disturb our tranquility of mind. In this branch of philosophy they were really great.
2. In developing our duties to others, they were short and defective. They embraced indeed the circles of kindred and friends, and inculcated patriotism, or the love of country in the aggregate, as a primary obligation: towards our neighbors and countrymen they taught justice, but scarcely viewed them as within the circle of benevolence. Still less have they inculcated peace, charity, and love to our fellow-men, or embraced with benevolence the whole family of mankind.

II. JEWS.

1. Their system was Deism, that is, the belief in one only God; but their ideas of him and of his attributes were degrading and injurious.
2. Their ethics were not only imperfect, but often irreconcilable with the sound dictates of reason and morality, as they respect intercourse with those around us; and repulsive and anti-social as respecting other nations. They needed reformation, therefore, in an eminent degree.

III. JESUS.

In this state of things among the Jews, Jesus appeared. His parentage was obscure; his condition poor; his education null; his natural endowments great; his life correct and innocent. He was meek, benevolent, patient, firm, disinterested, and of the sublimest eloquence. The disadvantages under which his doctrines appear are remarkable.

1. Like Socrates and Epictetus, he wrote nothing himself.

2. But he had not, like them, a Xenophon or an Arrian to write for him. I name not Plato, who only used the name of Socrates to cover the whimsies of his own brain.

On the contrary, all the learned of his country, entrenched in its power and riches, were opposed to him, lest his labors should undermind their advantages; and the committing to writing of his life and doctrines fell on unlettered and ignorant men; who wrote, too, from memory, and not till long after the transactions had passed.

3. According to the ordinary fate of those who attempt to enlighten and reform mankind, he fell an early victim to the jealousy and combination of the altar and the throne, at about 33 years of age, his reason having not yet attained the maximum of its energy, nor the course of his preaching, which was but of three years at most, presented occasions for developing a complete system of morals.

4. Hence the doctrines which he really delivered were defective, as a whole, and fragments only of what he did deliver have come to us mutilated, misstated, and often unintelligible.

5. They have been still more disfigured by the corruptions of schismatizing followers, who have found an interest in sophisticating and perverting the simple doctrines he taught, by engrafting on them the mysticisms of a Grecian Sophist (Plato), frittering them into subtitles and obscuring them with jargon, until they have caused good men to reject the whole in disgust, and to view Jesus himself as an imposter. Notwithstanding these disadvantages, a system of morals is presented to us which, if filled up in the true style and spirit of the rich fragments he left us, would be the most perfect and sublime that has ever been taught by man. The question of his being a member of the Godhead, or in direct communication with it, claimed for him by some of his followers, and denied by others, is foreign to the present view, which is merely an estimate of the intrinsic merits of his doctrines.

1. He corrected the Deism of the Jews, confirming them in their belief of one only god, and giving them juster notions of his attributes and government.

2. His moral doctrines, relating to kindred and friends, were more pure and perfect than those of the most correct of the philosophers, and greatly more so than those of the Jews; and they went far beyond both in inculcating universal philanthropy, not only to kindred and friends, to neighbors and countrymen, but to all mankind, gathering all into one family, under the bonds of love, charity, peace, common wants, and common aids. A development of this head will evince the peculiar superiority of the system of Jesus over all others.

3. The precepts of philosophy and of the Hebrew code laid hold of action only. ***He pushed his scrutinies into the heart of man; erected his tribunal in the region of his thought, and purified the waters at the fountain head.*** [Italics added].

4. He taught emphatically the doctrine of a future state, which was either doubted or disbelieved by the Jews; and wielded it with efficacy as an important incentive, supplementary to the other motives to moral conduct.

APPENDIX II

The following newspaper article, and the material in Appendices III, IV, and V, reveal the fascinating discovery, debate, and controversy that surrounded the Congressional publication of Jefferson's so-called "Bible."

St. Louis Globe-Democrat
May 20, 1900

JEFFERSON'S BIBLE.

An Exceedingly Interesting Book Unearthed in the National Library — A Compilation of the Moral Doctrines of Christ.

Washington, D.C., May 16 – Clergy and layman will be interested in knowing that through the diligent search of Representative Lacey, of Iowa, what is known as the "Jefferson Bible" has been brought to light. This little volume was compiled by Thomas Jefferson, and it contains the moral doctrines of Christ, the portions of the Scripture of a supernatural nature being omitted. So thoroughly did Jefferson go into this work that when it was completed the moral doctrines of the Savior were posted in a blank-book in parallel columns, being in the Greek, Latin, French, and English languages.

This interesting book is now in an iron safe at the National Museum and is under lock and key. But for the interest Judge Lacey took in the matter, this almost unknown and forgotten volume would have been entirely lost sight of. The story of this precious book is best told in the words of Judge Lacey, as follows:

Editor: Representative Lacey's "words" were repeated verbatim on the floor of the House to support his resolution to print the Jefferson "Bible" at government expense. See the May 10, 1902 Congressional Record in Appendix III, pages A-6 through A-9.

APPENDIX III

Congressional Record—House
January 7, 1902

REPORTS ON PRIVATE BILLS AND RESOLUTIONS.

By Mr. LACEY: A concurrent resolution (H.C. Res. 15) providing for the printing of Thomas Jefferson's Morals of Jesus of Nazareth—to the Committee on Printing.

Rep. John F. Lacey from Oskaloosa, Iowa

• • • • • • • • • •

May 10, 1902

MORALS OF JESUS OF NAZARETH, BY THOMAS JEFFERSON.

Mr. HEATWOLE. Mr. Speaker, I ask present consideration of the following privileged report:

Rep. Joel Heatwole from Northfield, Minnesota

The Clerk read as follows:

House concurrent resolution 15.

Resolved, etc., **That there be printed in facsimile for the use of Congress 9,000 copies of Thomas Jefferson's Morals of Jesus of Nazareth, as the same appears in the National Museum, 3,000 copies for the use of the Senate and 6,000 copies for the use of the House.**

The amendment recommended by the committee was read, as follows:

In the second line strikeout the words "in facsimile" and insert in lieu thereof "and bound, by photolithographic process, with an introduction of not to exceed 25 pages, to be prepared by Dr. Cyrus Adler, librarian of the Smithsonian Institution."

So that the resolution shall read as follows:

Resolved, etc., **That there be printed and bound, by photolithographic process, with an introduction of not to exceed 25 pages, to be prepared by Dr. Cyrus Adler, librarian of the Smithsonian Institution, for the use of Congress, 9,000 copies of Thomas Jefferson's Morals of Jesus of Nazareth, as the same appeared in the National Museum, 3,000 copies for the use of the Senate and 6,000 copies for the use of the House."**

The report is as follows:

Your Committee on Printing, having had under consideration House concurrent resolution No. 15, providing for the printing of 9,000 copies of Thomas Jefferson's Morals of Jesus of Nazareth, recommend that the same do pass with the following amendment.

In second line strikeout the words "in facsimile" and insert in lieu thereof "and bound, by photolithographic process, with

an introduction of not to exceed 25 pages, to be prepared by Dr. Cyrus Adler, librarian of the Smithsonian Institution."

So that the resolution shall read as follows:

***"Resolved, etc.,* That there be printed and bound, by photolithographic process, with an introduction of not to exceed 25 pages, to be prepared by Dr. Cyrus Adler, librarian of the Smithsonian Institution, for the use of Congress, 9,000 copies of Thomas Jefferson's Morals of Jesus of Nazareth, as the same appeared in the National Museum, 3,000 copies for the use of the Senate and 6,000 copies for the use of the House."**

The Public Printer estimates the cost of this work, exclusive of the proposed introduction, at $3,227.

The SPEAKER pro tempore. The question is on agreeing to the amendment.

Speaker: David B. Henderson from Dubuque, Iowa

Mr. GROSVENOR. Mr. Speaker, what is this?

Mr. HEATWOLE. I yield to the gentleman from Iowa.

Mr. LACEY. Mr. Speaker, Congress has published all the works of Thomas Jefferson with the exception of this volume, and that was not published because it was not then in the Congressional Library. Since then it has been added to the Library.

Mr. GROSVENOR. What is it?

Rep. Charles H. Grosvenor from Athens, Ohio

Mr. LACEY. "Morals of Jesus of Nazareth," as compiled by Thomas Jefferson. It makes a small volume, compiled textually from the four Gospels. This is a work of which there is only one copy in the world: and should it be lost, it would be a very great loss.

Mr. GROSVENOR: Would the gentleman consent to put Dillingworth's spelling book as an appendix to the work?

Mr. LACEY. That would be very amusing, Mr. Speaker; but this is really one of the most remarkable contributions of Thomas Jefferson.

Mr. GROSVENOR: Not more so than a great many other works of private enterprise by various individuals.

Mr. PAYNE. Why not substitute the four Gospels?

Rep. Sereno E. Payne from Auburn, New York

Mr. LACEY. The Government owns this manuscript, and it is the only copy in the world.

Mr. GROSVENOR. I wish it had never been found. [Laughter.]

Here begins Mr. Lacey's article that was published in the St. Louis Globe-Democrat on May 20, 1900.

Mr. LACEY. Mr. Speaker, there is a little volume of 164 pages in the library of the National Museum, bound in red morocco by a Richmond bookbinder, which is one of the curious things in Washington, that is rarely seen. Thomas Jefferson's library was purchased by the Government and is now contained in the splendid Congressional Library. Some time ago, in giving the Jefferson collection careful examination, I found that the "Jefferson Bible," as it is sometimes called, was not there. No one could tell me where it was until I asked A.R. Spofford, who knows everything about books, and he told me it was in the National Museum library. It appears that the volume was not included in the sale of Mr. Jefferson's library, but was afterwards purchased for $400 from Miss Randolph. This book is too valuable to be kept on the shelves of the Museum library, but Dr. Cyrus Adler keeps it under lock and key and carries the key himself.

Mr. Jefferson was a freethinker, but his clear and just mind appreciated the teachings of the founder of the Christian religion, and the study of the Scriptures was the frequent occupation of his busy mind. He read Marcus Aurelius, Epictetus, and other ancient writers on moral philosophy, and he conceived the idea of condensing the life and teachings of Jesus into a small volume, in which everything of a supernatural character should be omitted, evidently believing that the great truths of the religion of our Saviour would lose nothing by being separated from the miracles and wonders with which they are accompanied in the text of the Gospels.

John Adams and Mr. Jefferson, at one time bitter enemies, became in their retirement ardent friends, and were as regular in their correspondence as a pair of boarding-school girls. This compilation became the subject of their correspondence, and Mr. Jefferson promised to complete the work.

On January 20, 1804, in a letter written at Washington to Dr. Priestly, he said:

I rejoice that you have undertaken the task of comparing the moral doctrines of Jesus with those of the ancient philosophers.

I think you can not avoid giving, as a preliminary to the comparison, a digest of his moral doctrines, extracted in his own words from the Evangelists and leaving out everything relative to his personal history and character. It would be short and precious. With a view to do this for my own satisfaction, I had sent to Philadelphia to get two Greek testaments of the same edition and two English, with a design to cut the doctrines of morality and paste them on the leaves of a book in the manner you describe in framing your harmony. But I shall now get the thing done by better hands.

In his letter to Mr. Adams August 22, 1813, he says that he had prepared a syllabus of the Christian teachings for Dr. Priestly and Dr. Rush, and that Dr. Rush's family had returned it after the death of that gentleman, to Mr. Jefferson's great delight, for he found that it would involve him in a religious controversy.

On January 9, 1816, he wrote to Charles Thompson on the subject:

I, too, have made a little book from the same materials, which I call the Philosophy of Jesus. It is a paradigma of his doctrines, made by cutting the texts out of the books and arranging them on the pages of a blank book in a certain order of time or subject. A more beautiful or previous morsel of ethics I have never seen. * * * If I had time, I would add to my little book the Greek, Latin, and French texts in columns side by side.

On October 31, 1819, he wrote from Monticello to William Short:

As you may say of yourself, I too, am an epicurean. I consider the genuine (not the imputed) doctrines of Epicurus as containing everything rational in moral philosophy which Greece and Rome have left us. * * * But the greatest of all reformers of the depraved religion of his own country was Jesus of Nazareth. * * * Epictetus and Epicurus give laws for governing ourselves, Jesus a supplement of the duties and charities we owe to others. * * * I have sometimes thought of translating Epictetus (for he has never been tolerably translated into English) by adding the doctrines of Epictetus from the syntagma of Gassendi and an abstract from the Evangelists. * * * The last I attempted too hastily some twelve or fifteen years ago. It was the work of some two or three nights only, at Washington, after getting through the evening's task of reading the letters and papers of the day. But with one foot in the grave these are now idle projects for me.

Evidently Mr. Jefferson did resume the work and reproduced it with great care. The book is a duodecimo volume of 82 double pages, or 164 pages, though Mr. Jefferson has paged only the left-hand page. On the left hand he has pasted the clippings in two columns, first in Greek and then in Latin. On the right hand he has put the French version first and the English in the last column. So the whole is neatly pasted in four finely printed columns in Greek, Latin, French, and English. There are marginal notes in Jefferson's own handwriting, with a table in front giving the pages and citing the chapters and verses from which the clippings are taken. In his writings he says that he has sent for two Testaments in each language for the purpose. The scope of the book is indicated by the title page, which is in Jefferson's handwriting: The Life and Morals of Jesus of Nazareth, Extracted Textually from the Gospels in Greek, Latin, French, and English.

In a marginal note he gives the Roman law on sedition under which Jesus was tried. A map of Judea is attached, convenient for reference, and the whole work bears evidence of the compiler's care and characteristic neatness.

He has omitted everything of a miraculous nature and has confined his clippings to the pure teachings of Jesus. He has clipped from all the Gospels, using the verses which made the clearest statement where the texts are practically the same, but he inserts texts from all of them, so as to include the entire teachings of the Saviour. The result is unique. In a clear, lucid form, apart from all surroundings of the supernatural, appear the words and moral teachings of the Son of Man.

In the concluding verse of the work he takes John xix, 42, and Matthew xxvii, 60, and combines them, clipping out all but the plain statement of the burial. The result is as follows:

John xix, 42: There laid they Jesus, * * *

Matthew xxvii, 60: * * * and * * * rolled a great stone to the door of the sepulcher, and departed.

So he leaves Jesus buried forever in the grave and gives no hope of the "resurrection and the life."

Though it is a blue-penciled and expurgated New Testament, it has not been prepared in any irreverent spirit. The result is a consolidation of the beautiful, pure teachings of the Saviour in a compact form, mingled with only so much of narrative as a Virginia lawyer would hold to be credible in those matter-of-fact days, and the opportunity is given, plain and unadorned, to compare these teachings with Marcus Aurelius's and other pagan "morals." They are in striking contrast to Plutarch's morals, or rather, his immorals. ***No greater practical test of the worth of the tenets of the Christian religion could be made than the publication of this condensation by Mr. Jefferson. The jewels are taken from their settings, but they shine with their own luster. A verse of John is combined with a verse of Matthew with no interlineations, but is blended into a harmonious whole.*** [Italics added].

In these days of photolithography this little volume can be easily reproduced in facsimile. The work was intended to place the morals of Jesus in a form where, simple and alone, they could be contrasted with the teachings of the pagan philosophers. In doing this work Mr. Jefferson has builded better than he knew, and I trust that we may now have a reproduction of this beautiful little volume in a form to be accessible to the Christian world.

It has been said by an eminent minister of the gospel that Christianity must be true or it could never have survived so much poor preaching. Mr. Jefferson has put it to a still better test by this abridgement of the doctrines of the Divine Author.

Rep. Lacey completes the reading of his May 20, 1900 article.

The SPEAKER. The first question is on agreeing to the amendments.

The question was considered, and the amendments agreed to.

The resolution was agreed to.

Congressional Record—House
May 21, 1902

"THE MORALS OF JESUS OF NAZARETH."

Mr. LACEY. Mr. Speaker, I ask unanimous consent for the present consideration of the resolution which I send to the Clerk's desk.

The SPEAKER pro tempore. The gentleman from Iowa asks unanimous consent for the present consideration of a resolution which the Clerk will report.

The Clerk read as follows:

***Resolved by the House of Representatives (The Senate concurring),* Whereas it has been ascertained that the authorities of the National Museum Library have expressed their willingness to permit private parties to publish the volume in said library known as "The Morals of Jesus of Nazareth," by Thomas Jefferson, and that private publishers have expressed their purpose to do so, House concurrent resolution No. 15 of the present Congress is hereby rescinded.**

The SPEAKER pro tempore. Is there objection?

Mr. SHATTUC. Mr. Speaker, reserving the right to object, I should like to have the gentleman explain the purpose of the resolution.

Rep. William B. Shattuc from Madisonville, Ohio

Mr. LACEY. Mr. Speaker, at the request of a good many persons interested in the publication, I introduced the resolution which passed here the other day. Subsequent arrangements have been made by which this book will be published privately, and therefore there is no necessity for its publication by Congress.

Mr. WARNOCK. This is to be done without expense to the Government?

Rep. William R. Warnock from Urban, Ohio

Mr. LACEY. Without expense to the Government. That being the case, I simply ask to have the former resolution rescinded.

Mr. SHATTUC. Do we become responsible for its publication?

Mr. LACEY. Not at all. We simply withdraw this resolution, and private parties will publish it without any expense to the Government.

Mr. BALL of Texas. That is true of pretty nearly all the publications that we distribute, is it not, that private parties would publish them?

Rep. Thomas H. Ball from Huntsville, Texas

Mr. LACEY. The reason this was offered was because Congress had the control of the manuscripts in that collection, and this book not having been published, it was thought Congress ought to authorize this publication, as it had authorized the others; but as it will be published in any event, even if Congress has it printed, we might as well save the expense and let it be published by private parties.

Mr. BALL of Texas. If that is the purpose of this resolution, I object, Mr. Speaker.

The SPEAKER pro tempore. Objection is made.

The dialogue ends here with no further action taken.

May 22, 1902

REPORT OF COMMITTEES ON
PRIVATE BILLS AND RESOLUTIONS

By Mr. LACEY: A concurrent resolution (H.C. Res. 52) to rescind the passage of House concurrent resolution No. 15, authorizing the printing of "The Morals of Jesus of Nazareth," by Thomas Jefferson—to the Committee on Printing.

[See APPENDIX VII, Page A-22, where Cyrus Adler notes that H.C. Res. 52 received no consideration.]

APPENDIX IV
Richmond Dispatch
May 22, 1902—Thursday
Thomas Jefferson's Bible

Chairman Heatwole on Character of Book to Be Published by Congress.

Representative Heatwole, chairman of the House Committee on Printing, was asked Tuesday, says the *Washington Post,* the nature of the publication known as "The Morals of Jesus of Nazareth" prepared by Thomas Jefferson which Congress has recently ordered printed. He was also asked why Congress should be called on to have the work printed. In answer to the inquiry Mr. Heatwole said:

A great many years ago Congress purchased all of the books and manuscripts of Mr. Jefferson and placed them in the Library of Congress, and Congress has attempted the publication of all of the works of Mr. Jefferson, complete. This little volume was not published at the time of the authorized printing of Mr. Jefferson's works by Congress; it was not then in the collection. This book had been retained by Miss Randolph who is at present living at or near Charlottesville, Va, and she now has in her possession the four original copies of the Bibles from which the clippings were made. The book, which has excited more or less discussion during the last few days, was sold to Congress by Miss Randolph and is now in the National Museum, where it is kept as a curiosity.

Mr. Jefferson has been unjustly criticized in regard to this very book, and in justice to him it should be made public. Representative Lacey, of Iowa, about a year ago found the book under lock and key in the National Museum, and write a short article describing it, which was printed in many papers of the country, and the result is that frequent requests have been made for the publication of the book, these request coming largely from ministers of the Gospel on the one hand, and people interested in the memory of Thomas Jefferson on the other hand. Accordingly Mr. Lacey introduced a resolution in the House providing for the publication of the work. It was carefully considered by the House Committee on Printing and favorably reported. Mr. Jefferson, in his late years, was in frequent correspondence with John Adams, and in that correspondence Mr. Jefferson suggested the preparation of the morals of the Christian religion, collated verbatim from the four evangelists, and in the most reverent spirit he has prepared this little book. The effect of it is most excellent, and is one of the most convincing proofs of the Christian religion. He has prepared this little compendium in

Greek, Latin, French, and English. He has not used a single syllable or punctuation mark that is not taken literally from the Gospels. He has done it entirely without any words of his own. No one that examines this little volume, whether he is a saint or a sinner, will rise from his perusal without having a loftier idea of the teachings of the Saviour.

There is but one copy of the book in the world and that belongs to Congress. ***The object of having it printed was to lay the book open to the world, where it can do nothing but good.*** [Italics added.] There has been some misapprehension in some quarters as to the scope of this work, and any criticism upon this publication has been wholly upon misapprehension or lack of knowledge of what the book really contains. The preachers of the country are flooding Mr. Lacey, of Iowa, with requests for a copy of "Jefferson's Bible." They are writing me from everywhere," said the Iowan yesterday. "I have one request from Paris and another from as far West as Salt Lake City."

"There isn't even a semicolon in it," explained Mr. Lacey yesterday "that is not found in the Bible. The excuse for printing it now is that the government has printed all the works of Thomas Jefferson, except this one, which was owned by private parties when the other books were republished."

The Government Printing Office will not complete the work for some time yet.

APPENDIX V

Richmond Dispatch
May 27, 1902 Tuesday

Jefferson's "Bible"

Breeze Concerning House Direction to Print It

Publishers and Ministers Both Oppose the Printing, but for Different Reasons

Washington, D.C.—May 26—(Special)

There is quite a "breeze" between the publishing houses and the preachers over "Jefferson's Bible," nine thousand copies of which the House of Representatives has authorized to be printed. The preachers generally oppose the publication of the "Bible" by the government, and so do the publishers, the latter wanting the job for themselves. They wish to secure the printing privilege for general sale. They are, therefore, reinforcing the clergymen who are memorializing Congress to rescind its action regarding the printing of nine thousand copies. The protests of the ministers, who are said to be afraid of an erroneous impression of Jefferson's treatise on Christianity, continue to pour in, and the enterprising publishers are "pushing the game along" in the language of the street. A member of the House Committee on Printing, who is a proponent of the scheme to take the printing of the "Bible" out of the hands of Congress, said that in his judgment a million copies of the book could be sold at one dollar each, so widespread has become the interest in the work, which is among the treasured relics of the government in the Congressional Library.

The edition could be made most attractive and the publishers even then could make twenty-five cents per copy on every one sold. This would mean $250,000 net profit on a million copies. It is not at all probable that the effort will be made to have the House reconsider the vote by which the resolution ordering 9,000 copies printed was passed. But it is strongly doubtful if such a plan would succeed.

APPENDIX VI

CYRUS ADLER'S "INTRODUCTION" TO THE 1904 EDITION OF JEFFERSON'S BIBLE [1]

The so-called Jefferson Bible, more accurately "The Life and Morals of Jesus of Nazareth," is now the property of the United States National Museum at Washington, having been obtained by purchase in 1895...

That Jefferson had in mind the preparation of such a book, and that he actually prepared it, has been known to students of his letters and writings, and especial attention was drawn to the fact in "The Life and Times of Thomas Jefferson," by Henry S. Randall, published in three volumes, New York, 1858.

It was, moreover, brought to the attention of the Government very definitely in the form of a report, Fifty-first Congress, First Session, Senate Report 1365, presented June 14, 1890, by Senator Evarts of the Committee on Library, and ordered printed. This report was with reference to a bill relative to the proposed purchase of the manuscript papers and correspondence of Thomas Jefferson, which does not appear to have been followed by favorable action. In it the following description is given of the book in question, which was written by Mr. Ainsworth R. Spofford, then Librarian of Congress:

"*The Morals and Life of Jesus of Nazareth,* extracted textually from the Gospels in Greek, Latin, French and English. Title and very full index in his own hand. Texts were cut by him out of printed copies of Greek, Latin, French and English Testaments and pasted in this book of blank pages, which was handsomely bound in red morocco, ornamented in gilt, and titled on the back in gilt letters, 'The Morals of Jesus.' His original idea was to have the life and teachings of the Saviour, told in similar excerpts, prepared for the Indians, thinking this simple form would suit them best. But, abandoning this, the formal execution of his plan took the shape above described, which was for his individual use. He used the four languages that he might have the texts in them side by side, convenient for comparison. In the book he pasted a map of the ancient world and the Holy Land, with which he studied the New Testament."...

1. Mr. Adler's historical "Introduction" is very significant to the story of Jefferson's "Bible." But his understanding in 1904 was limited in certain aspects, leading to a few factual mistakes. Some of these errors are noted in parentheses. The ellipses indicate the removal of extraneous material and digressions by Mr. Adler that are unimportant to the historical account.

I undertook to search for the volumes, first through Miss Sarah N. Randolph, who, just as I was about to call on her on the subject, died, and, after a lapse of some years and with steps that it is not necessary to detail, obtained it from Miss Randolph, her sister, then living at Shadwell, Va. The latter, in a communication dated July 27, 1895, states of Jefferson that "the idea he had at first was to compile a book which would be valuable for the use of the Indians."

This little book was one which occupied a great deal of Jefferson's attention, and the following statements and extracts from his letters directly bear upon its making.

On April 9, 1803, he wrote from Washington to Dr. Priestley, referring to Priestley's comparative view of Socrates and Jesus, that in a conversation with Dr. Rush in the years 1798 and 1799 he had promised some day to write a letter giving his view of the Christian system. This letter he had as yet only sketched out in his mind. It was evident that he considered the Gospels as having much extraneous matter and that by careful pruning there could be selected out those sayings which were absolutely the words of Jesus himself. After discussing the injustice done by these later additions, he says to Priestley, "you are the person who of all others would do it best and most promptly. You have all the materials at hand, and you put together with ease. I wish you could be induced to extend your late work to the whole subject."

In a letter of ten days later, April 19, 1803, to Edward Dowse, he writes that he considers "the moral precepts of Jesus as more pure, correct and sublime than those of the ancient philosophers."

Under date of April 21, 1803, Jefferson wrote to Dr. Benjamin Rush, sending him the syllabus of an estimate of the merits of the doctrines of Jesus compared with those of others. This is the communication to which he had referred in his letter to Dr. Priestley. In the letter accompanying the syllabus he tells Dr. Rush that he is sending this for his own eye, simply in performance of his promise, and indicates its confidential character . . .

On January 29, 1804, Jefferson wrote to Priestley from Washington that he was rejoiced to hear that Priestley had undertaken to compare the moral doctrines of Jesus with those of the ancient philosophers. He writes: "I think you cannot avoid giving, as preliminary to the comparison, a digest of his moral doctrines, extracted in his own words from the Evangelists, and leaving out everything relative to his personal history and character. It would be short and precious. With a view to do this for my own satisfaction, I had sent to Philadelphia to get two testaments (Greek) of the same edition, and two English, with a design to cut out the morsels of morality, and paste them on the leaves of a book, in the manner you describe as having been pursued in forming your Harmony. But I shall now get the thing done by better hands." [By Priestley himself.]

This is the first definite statement of Jefferson's purpose to prepare such a book, which he apparently at the time abandoned in the hope that Priestley would take it up. [Apparently Adler was unaware that Priestley died a week after Jefferson's letter, on February 6. Jefferson completed his compilation in February and had it bound by John Marsh on March 10, 1804]. In the year 1808 Jefferson was greatly interested in the translation of the Septuagint made by Charles Thomson, the Secretary of the first Continental Congress, and wrote several communications to Thomson on the subject. In 1813 John Adams began a voluminous correspondence with Jefferson on religious subjects, the letters following each other very closely. Adams had access to a number of Priestley's letters written to various persons and in a communication dated at Quincy, July 22, 1813, he reminds Jefferson of his intention of preparing the work which he (Jefferson) had handed over to Priestley [Adler is referring to Jefferson's "Syllabus" (See Appendix I)]. He writes: "I hope you will still perform your promise to Dr. Rush. If Priestley had lived, I should certainly have corresponded with him."

On August 9, John Adams again writes to Jefferson, sending further extracts of letters of Priestley and saying that he did so because "I wish it may stimulate you to pursue your own plan which you promised to Dr. Rush."

In a letter to Adams written from Monticello, October 12, 1813, Jefferson gives a description of the volume as follows: "We must reduce our volume to the simple Evangelists, select, even from them, the very words only of Jesus, paring off the amphiboligisms into which they have been led, by forgetting often, or not understanding, what had fallen from him, by giving their own misconceptions as his dicta, and expressing unintelligibly for others what they had not understood themselves. There will be found remaining the most sublime and benevolent code of morals which has ever been offered to man. I have performed this operation for my own use, by cutting verse by verse out of the printed book, and arranging the matter which is evidently his and which is as easily distinguished as diamonds in a dung-hill. The result is an octavo of forty-six pages."...

Under date of January 29, 1815, Jefferson wrote from Monticello to Charles Clay: "Probably you have heard me say I had taken the four Evangelists, had cut out from them every text they had recorded of the moral precepts of Jesus, and arranged them in a certain order, and although they appeared but as fragments, yet fragments of the most sublime edifice of morality which had ever been exhibited to man." In this letter however Jefferson disclaims any intention of publishing this little compilation, saying: "I not only write nothing on religion, but rarely permit myself to speak on it."

Again, in a letter to Charles Thomson, written from Monticello, under date of January 9, 1816, he says: "I, too, have made a wee little book from the same materials, which I call the Philosophy of Jesus; it is a paradigma of his doctrines, made by cutting the texts out of the book, and arranging them on the pages of a blank book, in a certain order of time or subject. A more beautiful or precious morsel of ethics I have never seen; it is a document in proof that I am a *real Christian*, that is to say, a disciple of the doctrines of Jesus."

Later in the letter Jefferson makes a statement which indicates that he is not describing the volume now in the National Museum, but the preliminary one of 46 pages, for he adds: "If I had time I would add to my little book the Greek, Latin and French texts, in columns side by side."

In a letter dated April 25, 1816, written from Poplar Forest, near Lynchburg, addressed to Mr. Fr. Adr. Vanderkemp, Jefferson gives further details as to how he made this preliminary volume. After telling his correspondent that he was very cautious about not having the syllabus, which he had prepared, get out in connection with his name, being unwilling to draw on himself "a swarm of insects, whose buzz is more disquieting than their bite," he writes: "I made, for my own satisfaction, an extract from the Evangelists of the text of His morals, selecting those only whose style and spirit proved them genuine, and his own. * * *It was too hastily done, however, being the work of one or two evenings only, while I lived at Washington, overwhelmed with other business, and it is my intention to go over it again at more leisure. This shall be the work of the ensuing winter. I gave it the title of 'The Philosophy of Jesus Extracted from the Text of the Evangelists.'"

Vanderkemp was undertaking a publication and desired to use Jefferson's syllabus and extract, which Jefferson agreed to, with the following condition: "I ask only one condition, that no possibility shall be admitted of my name being even intimated with the publication."

October 31, 1819, he writes from Monticello to William Short, speaking of the extract form the Evangelists and his desire to see a proper one made: "The last I attempted too hastily some twelve or fifteen years ago. It was the work of two or three nights only, at Washington, after getting through the evening task of reading the letters and papers of the day."

This concludes the references in Jefferson's writings that bear directly upon the little volume in question. They are brief extracts from a collection made from all sources, published and manuscript.

Randall, in his *Life of Jefferson,* already quoted, volume 3, page 451, says: "It was in the winter of 1816–17, it is believed, that Mr. Jefferson carried out the design last expressed [Historian

Randall was in error here. It was the winter of 1819-20]. In a handsome morocco-bound volume, labeled on the back, 'Morals of Jesus,' he placed the parallel texts in four languages. The first collection of English texts, mentioned in the letter to Thomson, is not preserved in Mr. Jefferson's family, but his grandson, Mr. George Wythe Randolph, has obtained for us a list of its contents. That, in different languages, is in the possession of his oldest grandson, Colonel Thomas Jefferson Randolph." Randall gives a list of the passages of both volumes in his appendix, and adds, "It is remarkable that neither of these collections were known to Mr. Jefferson's grandchildren until after his death. They then learned from a letter addressed to a friend that he was in the habit of reading nightly from them before going to bed."

It would appear from the letter to Short that Randall's deduction as to the date of this larger compilation is not warranted and that it was actually made in 1819 or subsequent to that year, although it is true that in the letter to Vanderkemp (April 25, 1816) he speaks of the larger compilation as being the work of the ensuing winter.

In Appendix No. XXX to Randall's work, he gives the list of the contents of the first compilation of forty-six pages as well as the list of the contents of the present book. These are not exactly identical. It is interesting to note the title of the first compilation, which reads as follows:

"THE PHILOSOPHY OF JESUS OF NAZARETH"

"Extracted from the account of his life and doctrines as given by Matthew, Mark, Luke and John. Being an abridgment of the New Testament for the use of the Indians, unembarrassed with matters of fact or faith beyond the level of their comprehensions."

The National government had purchased Mr. Jefferson's papers and had published an edition of his writings. Considerable interest was expressed in the so-called Bible after it came into the possession of the United States National Museum, and it was in consequence of this interest that the present compilation is published.

It is printed in pursuance to the following concurrent resolution adopted by the Fifty-seventh Congress, first session:

"That there be printed and bound, by photolithographic process, with an introduction of not to exceed twenty-five pages, to be prepared by Dr. Cyrus Adler, Librarian of the Smithsonian Institution, for the use of Congress, 9,000 copies of Thomas Jefferson's Morals of Jesus of Nazareth, as the same appears in the National Museum; 3,000 copies for the use of the Senate and 6,000 copies for the use of the House."

— *Cyrus Adler*

APPENDIX VII

Cosmopolitan
January, 1905
Volume 28, Pages 340–344

The Jefferson Bible

By CYRUS ADLER

Thomas Jefferson has been associated in the minds of his fellow citizens with the Declaration of Independence, with diplomacy, with the presidency, with scientific pursuits and with the University of Virginia, but never with religion except by way of denunciation as an atheist and freethinker. Nevertheless, it has long been known to students of Jefferson's letters, or to the reader of the excellent biography by Randall, that Jefferson himself had an intense interest in religion, that he was a student of the Gospels, and that he compiled one, in fact, two little volumes which contained, according to his view, the essence of the moral teachings of the New Testament. One of these books, now in the United States National Museum at Washington, is the second and more elaborate which he made. It is, externally, a little volume eight and a quarter inches high, nearly five inches wide, and about one inch and a half thick, bound in full red leather, labeled on the back "Morals of Jesus," with a statement on the inside left cover that it was "bound by Fred A. Mayo, Richmond, Virginia." The contents of the first part of this book are two leaves in the handwriting of Jefferson, containing a list of the texts employed in the book, a title-page in Jefferson's handwriting, reading "The Life and Morals of Jesus of Nazareth, extracted textually from the Gospels in Greek, Latin, French, and English," and two printed maps of Palestine and Asia Minor. The body of the book, which is on numbered leaves, running from 1 to 83, consists of extracts from the Gospels, on the left-hand pages in Greek and Latin and on the right in French and English. The sources are indicated in the margin in Jefferson's handwriting, but there is no annotation of any kind except on leaf 77, where he cites, probably inaccurately, the passage from the Roman law under which he supposes Jesus to have been tried.

I secured the book for the United States National Museum by purchase from Miss Randolph, of Shadwell, Virginia, in 1895, as the result of the following circumstance: In 1886, when a fellow of the Johns Hopkins University in Baltimore, I was engaged in cataloguing a valuable Hebrew library gathered together by the late Dr. Joshua I. Cohen. Amongst the books were two copies of the New Testament in English, mutilated, with a statement which indicated that they had belonged to Jefferson. The title-pages of these two books showed that they had been printed in Philadelphia in 1804. After following up various clues, the original was at length found in the possession of a member of the Jefferson family, as above stated.

From his correspondence with Doctor Priestley, the discoverer of oxygen, with Dr. Benjamin Rush, and many others, it is known that Jefferson early held the view that the Gospels contained later and extraneous matter, and on January 29, 1804, he wrote to Priestley that he was rejoiced to hear that he, Priestley, had undertaken to compare the moral doctrines of Jesus with those of the ancient philosophers, adding: "I think you cannot avoid giving, as preliminary to the comparison, a digest of his moral doctrines, extracted in his own words from the evangelists and leaving out everything relative to his personal history and character. It would be short and precious. With a view to do this for my own satisfaction, I had sent to Philadelphia to get two Testaments (Greek) of the same edition, and two English, with a design to cut out the morsels of morality, and paste them on the leaves of a book, in the manner you describe as having been pursued in forming your Harmony. But I shall now get the thing done by better hands."

About 1813, John Adams commenced a correspondence with Jefferson, reminding him of this work that he had intended to undertake, and in a letter to Adams from Monticello, October 12, 1813, Jefferson gives a description of the volume which he had prepared in the following words. "We must reduce our volume to the simple evangelists, select, even from them, the very words only of Jesus, paring off the amphibologisms into which they have been led, by forgetting often, or not understanding, what had fallen from him, by giving their own misconceptions as his dicta, and expressing unintelligibly for others what they had not understood themselves. There will be found remaining the most sublime and benevolent code of morals which has ever been offered to man. I have performed this operation for my own use, by cutting verse by verse out of the printed book, and arranging the matter which is evidently his, and which is as easily distinguishable as diamonds in a dunghill. The result is an octavo of forty-six pages."

The book here referred to is not at present known to be in existence. According to Randall, the title of this first compilation reads as follows: "The Philosophy of Jesus of Nazareth extracted from the account of his life and doctrines as given by Matthew, Mark, Luke, and John, being an abridgment of the New Testament for the use of the Indians, unembarrassed with matters of fact or faith beyond the level of their comprehensions." Although this volume is not known to be preserved, its contents, which differ slightly from the latter collection, are printed in the work of Randall already alluded to. The reason given for the making of the compilation, namely, that it was for the use of the Indians, is an extremely significant one, casting as it does a new light upon the breadth of Jefferson's interests.

Jefferson expresses his own opinion of the value of this compilation in a letter of January 29, 1815, dated at Monticello, to Charles Clay, in which he describes the collection as consisting of the "fragments of the most sublime edifice of morality which has ever been exhibited to man." In a letter to Charles Thompson, the Secretary of the Continental Congress, who himself had made a translation of the Bible, Jefferson wrote, under date of January 9, 1816: "I, too, have made a wee little book from the same materials, which I call the Philosophy of Jesus; it is a paradigma of his doctrines, made by cutting the texts out of the book, and arranging them on the pages of a blank book, in a certain order of time or subject. A more beautiful or precious morsel of ethics I have never seen; it is a document in proof that I am a real Christian, that is to say, a disciple of the doctrines of Jesus." It is plain, from the concluding statement in this letter, that he is still speaking of the early compilation of forty-six pages, for he adds, "If I had time, I would add to my little book the Greek, Latin, and French texts in columns side by side."

On April 25, 1816, he wrote from Poplar Forest, near Lynchburg, to Mr. Vanderkemp, that the first compilation was too hastily made, "being the work of one or two evenings only, while I lived in Washington, overwhelmed with business"; and on October 31, 1819, he wrote from Monticello to William Short: "The last I attempted too hastily some twelve or fifteen years ago. It was the work of two or three nights only, at Washington, after getting through the evening task of reading the letters and papers of the day." From these letters, it appears that, although Jefferson had intended to make a larger book in the winter of 1816–17, he had no yet done so in 1819, and that therefore the volume now in the National Museum was made in the winter of 1819, or subsequent thereto.

The volume has attracted a considerable interest, and in view of the fact that the government had published the other works of Jefferson, Congress passed a resolution to print the so-called Bible in facsimile. Objection was made to this resolution, under the mistaken notion that the compilation was an annotated one, which might be objectionable to some persons, and a resolution was introduced to rescind the order to print, but it received no consideration and the work is now being issued for the use of Congress.

It remains but to say that, in spite of the reason given by Jefferson for the preparation of this collection, its usefulness for the Indians,[1] there is discernible an empirical sort of New Testament criticism, and it would seem that this remarkable man, who was patriot, diplomatist, scholar and scientific man all in one, anticipated the theories of modern New Testament scholars as to the existence of an earlier or synoptic gospel, and that he actually prepared one for himself—the rude forerunner of later critical attempts. That he must have done this in a spirit of devotion, is evidenced by his letters, and by statements gathered from his family, as well as by the information derived from a letter addressed to a friend, in which he says that he was "in the habit of reading nightly from them [the two compilations] before going to bed."

---

1. Mr. Adler is in error on this point. Jefferson's 1820 work, ***The Life and Morals of Jesus of Nazareth***, did not have an educational purpose for the Indians, only the 1804 compilation did.

APPENDIX VIII

BIOGRAPHICAL SKETCH: JOHN F. LACEY (R-IOWA)

U.S. Representative John F. Lacey was a man of moral convictions, a man devoted to God, family, and country. The Biological Dictionary of the American Congress, 1774–1971, chronicles the following highlights of his life:

> Lacey, John Fletcher, a Representative from Iowa; born in New Martinsville, Va. (now West Virginia), May 30, 1841; moved to Iowa in 1855 with his parents, who settled in Oskaloosa; attended the common schools and pursued classical studies; engaged in agricultural pursuits; learned the trades of bricklaying and plastering; during the Civil War enlisted in Company H, Third Regiment, Iowa Volunteer Infantry, in May 1861 and afterward served in Company D, Thirty-third Regiment, Iowa Volunteer Infantry, as sergeant major, and as lieutenant in Company C of that regiment: promoted to assistant adjutant general on the staff of Brig. Gen. Samuel A. Rice, and after that officer was killed in battle was assigned to duty on the staff of Maj. Gen. Frederick Steele; studied law; was admitted to the bar in 1865 and commenced practice in Oskaloosa, Iowa; member of the House of Representatives in Iowa in 1870; elected city councilman in 1880; served one term as city solicitor; temporary chairman of the Republican State convention in 1898; served on the city council 1880–1883; elected as a Republican to the Fifty-first Congress (March 4, 1889–March 3, 1891); unsuccessful candidate for re-election; elected to the Fifty-third and to the six succeeding Congresses (March 4, 1893–March 3, 1907); was an unsuccessful candidate for re-election; resumed the practice of law; died in Oskaloosa, Iowa, September 29, 1913; interment in Forest Cemetery.[1]

The man himself is revealed by tributes from friends and colleagues after his death:[2]

"His ability was best exercised as a congressman. There he was recognized as one of the ablest men in Congress at a time when Congress was composed of able statesmen. He was an orator as well as a statesman and in extemporaneous speaking few were his equal...He was temperate and of clean personal habits, he had the highest regard for his word, which was regarded as good as his bond."

— James Powell in the Ottumwa *Courier*

"He was an influential man in Congress, a prodigious worker...an able lawyer, a forceful man in debate, a willing bearer of responsibility."

— Hon. George D. Perkins in the Sioux City *Journal*

"Mr. Lacey was a fine type of gentleman whom it was a genuine pleasure to know. Even his most pronounced political opponents felt a deep-seated esteem for him — an esteem that could not be blotted by all the turmoil of heated political campaigns. He was one of the ablest of the old guard of Iowa republicanism. And he was as uncompromising in his opposition to parties and principles in which he did not believe, as he was able."

— Cedar Rapids *Gazette*

"In all his life there has been little to criticize, but much to praise...His private life was pure and simple, without stain. In public life he was the soul of honor, a tireless, intelligent worker, a statesman who was to place the public good above private advantage. He had a depth of human sympathy seldom surpassed, and his unfailing cheerfulness and loyalty to justice and right, made and kept friends through his entire life. Probably no man in public life during his generation had a broader or more comprehensive view of public affairs and no man ever gave more cheerfully of his strength and time to secure useful legislation."

— Hon. W.G. Ray in the *Grinnell Herald*

"He was always well dressed and I never saw him save in a tightly buttoned Prince Albert coat of dark material. He was polite in manner and his agreeable address was well calculated to ingratiate him in the favor of any company in which he might be placed...He was the kind of a husband and father that God intended man to be: kind, loving, devoted, and pure. [He and wife Martha were the parents of four children: Eleanor, Raymond Fletcher, Marion, and Bernice.]...Never was a needy one turned from the door of the Lacey home empty-handed."

— James M. Mansfield
(Raised by the Lacey family)

Representative John Lacey exemplified many Godly attributes that Thomas Jefferson identified in his *Life and Morals of Jesus of Nazareth* as foundational virtues for good government, good citizenship, and for the survival of the American Republic. Is it any wonder that Mr. Lacey desired a "reproduction of the beautiful little volume in a form to be accessible to the Christian world"?

---

1. ***Biographical Dictionary of the American Congress, 1774–1971.*** (Washington, D.C., U.S. Government Printing Office, 1971), p. 1253.

2. The quotes are taken from a memorial volume of ***Major John Lacey*** (Cedar Rapids, IA: Iowa Park and Forestry Association, 1915), pp. 32–35. This book honors Lacey's pioneering work in conservation.

APPENDIX IX

Thomas Jefferson's Religious Beliefs[1]

by John Eidsmore
Professor of Constitutional Law
Faulkner University

The following nine points can be concluded about Jefferson's beliefs:

1. Thomas Jefferson was neither a deist nor an orthodox Christian; his views best conform to the Unitarians of his day.

2. Jefferson had faith in the power of human reason to apprehend truth and govern the affairs of men.

3. Jefferson's concept of God was monotheistic; he rejected trinitarianism as contrary to human reason. He regarded God as the Creator and Sustainer of the universe, as the author of natural and moral laws, as the giver of human rights and liberties, and as the beneficial and just judge of the universe who actively guides, superintends, and intervenes in human affairs.

4. Jefferson did not believe in Jesus Christ as the Son of God or as the Second Person of the Godhead, but he respected Jesus as the world's greatest example and teacher of morals.

5. Jefferson rejected the Bible as the inspired Word of God. He believed the Bible contained basic moral teachings of Jesus, but also believed it contained much which had been written later and which had to be rejected as false and contrary to reason.

6. Jefferson believed God created man as a free and rational creature; therefore no church or government may coerce human volition or interfere with liberty of conscience.

7. His emphasis on human freedom and human reason led him to oppose the predestination doctrines and theocratic practices of the Calvinists. Jefferson's belief that Jesus was originally monotheistic and that trinitarianism had been created later by the church, led him to oppose clergymen who were so concerned about church doctrine and church practice that they neglected the pure and simple moral teachings of Jesus. Jefferson eventually saw the value of Christianity for the nation and the individual; he attended church, gave to the support of several churches, and lived a pious life.

8. Jefferson rejected orthodox Christianity earlier in his life. In the 1790s he understood Christianity in terms of following the moral teachings of Jesus; in that respect he considered himself a Christian.

9. Jefferson believed religion was a private matter between a man and his God. Consequently, he was reluctant to offer his opinion on certain religious doctrines. For this reason it is difficult to confirm what Jefferson actually believed.

---

1. John Eidsmore, ***Christianity and the Constitution.*** (Grand Rapids, MI: Baker Books), pp. 245–256.

APPENDIX X

INDEX OF SCRIPTURES

MATTHEW .... PAGE(S)

MARK .... PAGE(S)

LUKE .... PAGE(S)

APPENDIX XI

INDEX OF MORAL PRINCIPLES*

"The most sublime and benevolent code of morals which has ever been offered to man."
— Thomas Jefferson
October 12, 1813

* This list is not meant to be exhaustive. Other moral principles, especially from the parables, can be found in Jefferson's "Bible."

APPENDIX XII

INDEX OF PARABLES

Parable – A story used to teach a moral or truth

Parables by Book:

Matthew	15
Mark	4
Luke	19
Total	38